COMPROMISED
A True Story
About Taking Back
A Stolen Childhood

BARBARA JEAN AUGUST

AUTHOR'S NOTE

This book is based on my personal recollections, memories, and interpretations of events that occurred during my childhood and throughout the course of my life. Other individuals may have differing recollections, memories, and interpretations. I intend no harm to anyone as a result of the writing and publications of this book.

ISBN-13: 978-1548220662
ISBN-10: 1548220663

DEDICATION

To Harold,
my strongest supporter and confidant,

and to the survivors of child sexual abuse
around the world.

CONTENTS

ACKNOWLEDGMENTS

My heartfelt thanks and deepest appreciation to each of the following:

Elaine Thomas. Without you, I would never have started this book. You put my story on paper via our phone interviews and that was the beginning of a two-and-a-half-year journey. I am forever grateful.

Vicki Roy. Thank you for believing in me and supporting what you knew to be an important topic.

Barbara Hopkins. Your friendship, support, and encouragement helped me believe that I needed to do this. Your insight lets me know how important it was to write this book. I value our conversations and collaboration on the topic of this book.

Dr. Eric Lewis. My health issues of a very sensitive nervous system came to light when I met you. You answered so many questions and related the cumulative effects of my compromised nervous system to my past. I would never have considered that, if not for you.

Mark Love. Thank you for taking the time to give me the websites and statistics I needed to place at the end of my book, identifying the enormous problem of child predators.

Father Ed Kucera, Jr. Your blessings, prayers, encouragement and friendship mean more than you know.

Ed Robertson. You took my manuscript and rearranged it in a way to tell a story from a writer's, editor's, and reader's point of view. You are a

Godsend. We've shared a lot and it's made a lasting imprint on my life. There will always be a connection.

Lastly, my husband, *Harold*. This book would not have been possible without your support, encouragement, and love.

All of you have helped me write something that, two and a half years ago, seemed so monumental and hard to even imagine being able to accomplish. Writing this book put into perspective the journey of my life in order to continue on as a child advocate and possibly help others.

There are currently many organizations today, working with and helping to make a difference in the awareness of child abuse and protection for children. I have financially supported some of these organizations and now hope to work with them as a child advocate.

*The influence of a mother in the lives of her children
is beyond calculation.*

~James E. Faust

*The test of the morality of a society
is what it does for its children.*

~Dietrich Bonhoeffer

PROLOGUE

The last memory I have of my father is when my mother got a phone call. I was three and a half years old at the time. I knew something had happened when she went into the bedroom and lay down on the bed crying, but I didn't know what was wrong. Then she got up and got out his shirt, his suit, his tie and his black and white wing tip shoes. When a man came to the door, she handed him these things. He gave her back the shoes.

My father died in July 1948 at the age of forty-two. He had a fatal heart attack, which has been a huge health issue for the men on my father's side of the family. Grandfathers to cousins, they have all had their share of heart problems, a genetic weakness. The funeral service was at St. Patrick's Catholic Church in Honolulu, where we went to Mass every Sunday, and he was buried at Diamond Head Memorial Cemetery. I remember the funeral because they lowered the casket into the ground and put the dirt on it while we stood there. In those days that was how it was done.

I had siblings. My brother, whom I'll call Dallas, was born in 1947. He was a year and a half younger than I was. A sister, whom I'll call Jersey, was born nine days before my father died. We ended up staying with various people while my mother figured out what she was going to do. I went to live with my godparents, Ludy and Joe Rodriguez. They had two children, Robert and Carol. I adored them. They were very kind people. Joe had only one arm. They also lived in Honolulu.

My brother went to stay with my Aunty Rita and Uncle Adolph. My sister stayed with my maternal grandmother, Ida.

I don't know how long I was with Ludy and Joe, but I remember wishing I could live there forever. I now wonder why I wanted to live with them and not my mother. Soon you'll understand why.

The next memory I have is when I was about four years old and we were at Aunty Helen's for a get-together. In Hawaii, all older people are called "aunty" or "uncle" as a sign of respect. They didn't have to be relatives.

At this particular get-together was a man who was a friend of my mother's. He was in his early twenties, about ten years younger than she. He seemed nice, until he picked me up and set me on his lap. I was wearing a little short dress and he had his hands just under my dress, rubbing my legs. I didn't like it. I wanted to get down. I tried to push him away, but he kept me there.

I may have been just four years old, but my instincts told me that I did not want to be around him. I began making childish gestures, doing everything I could to resist him, until my Aunty Helen finally noticed and said, "You go and play with the children."

Whether she saw something, or sensed that something wasn't right, I don't know, but I got the impression that she didn't like me sitting there, either. When I went to play with the rest of the kids, I made sure I avoided this man for the rest of the day.

That was before he married my mother. Looking back, I think that little get-together was an engagement party or something to that effect. I don't know exactly how long they knew each other, but my stepfather and my mother married each other on August 6, 1949, a little more than a year after my father died.

* * *

I continued to avoid my stepfather because I did not like the man. I would wake up at night and find him standing over my bed, with my covers pulled down. He'd try to pet me, so to speak, but I would always make noise and say, "No." Then he'd turn and walk past my sister's bed, but he'd never stay there. He would leave.

One time, I had gone into the backyard to do something. I don't remember what. I was near the chicken coop that was fenced in and located behind the garage, when suddenly I realized he was out there. He made me come into that covered area. I did not want to be alone with him, but he made me go inside.

He exposed himself and placed my hand on his penis. I pulled it back and said, "No," and then, of course, he had a climax that went all over my leg. I didn't know what it was. I had no clue. I ran from there and ran into my mother.

She said, "What are you doing?"

I told her, "I'm going in the house."

She put her arm out and stopped me. Then she saw the semen on me.

"What's that?" she said.

"I don't know," I told her.

My mother had to know what my stepfather had done to me. She had to. But she didn't do anything about it. Though I didn't know it at the time, it would be up to me to finally make him stop.

* * *

This is a memoir of sadness, grief, strength, endurance and, above all, faith.

I struggled for a long time over whether to write this book. Would anyone want to read my story and what would be the ultimate purpose? The ultimate purpose could be to help those who have gone through, and survived, sexual abuse and to know there can be lifelong mental and medical repercussions if you simply bury what happened and think you can just move on. At some point, as you age, you will have to deal with those repercussions, whether you want to or not.

I have four grown siblings who have wrestled with what my stepfather did to us well into their senior years. Fortunately, I learned how to deal with it a long time ago, as you will read. Even from a young age, I refused to let what happened to me define me for the rest of my life. I was going to win, no matter what. Somehow I just had that mindset.

Yet still, one question gnawed at me: "Why did my mother not protect us?"

For decades I speculated there must have been an underlying reason I didn't know about. In recent years, that question was answered, but not in a way I expected. As this story unfolds you will know what I know and still have a hard time understanding it.

What does it mean to be a mother? How does a mother affect her children: Are there lifelong scars left when a mother is not a mother?

True, we can just as easily ask these questions of any father, especially since in today's society some men take on the role of nurturer, while women become the provider. However, throughout human history, it has been the natural inherent responsibility of the mother to care for and protect her children. While a father provides care and protection to his family, it is the actions, care, and responsibility of a mother that impact her children, for better or worse, throughout their entire lives. So whether a female assumes the role, or a male, the mother figure is the building block for the child.

I say all this to show the unbelievable repercussion that my mother had on her children. I know that many others have experienced the kind of sexual abuse I went through as a child. I have also learned, through my own studies and analysis, that the No. 1 reason why most victims of child abuse often won't discuss it is fear of repercussion. This is particularly true if, for some reason, they are not removed from the abusive setting. (And in cases where sexual abuse is involved, that can be even more devastating to an individual because there are no outward signs—it's all internal.)

If you're one such person, or if you know someone who has survived similar trauma involving physical, mental or sexual abuse, I wrote this book in hopes that you might gain insight from my experience and realize that you are not alone. Perhaps it might help you find the strength to talk about it, if you've never come forward before.

My friend Barbara is a licensed clinical social worker with a graduate degree in child psychology. She knows every detail of my story and will offer her own analysis later on in these pages. She once said to me, "In our industry, you are the phenomenon, because you are not anything like the rest of your siblings." She encouraged me to write the book, if only to answer the questions "How does that happen? What is that difference?"

For me, as you'll see, the only real answer is because I had a lot of faith. I did. It really was as if someone was helping me along whenever I needed it most.

I suspect there are many individuals living what seems like a normal to average life, in the eyes of other people, yet they harbor so many questions in relationship to their abnormal life as children. What does it all mean? Why did it happen to me? Where do I go from here? What is God's role in all of this?

I offer you my story as a window into a life from childhood to adolescence to adulthood with all the life situations involving family and the repercussions of this lifelong drama on the long-term effects of child sexual abuse. In doing so I hope to foment a new awareness about the devastating impact that sexual abuse has on children for the rest of their lives.

Children are the future of our society. We really need to protect them, as children.

The author, age three and a half, with her Aunt Ludy

View of Diamond Head Memorial Cemetery,
where the author's father is buried

CHAPTER ONE
The Family History

My father was Joe and my mother was Irene. On my father's side, I am a second-generation native of Hawaii; on my mother's side, I am a third-generation native of Hawaii. My mother's family came from the Madeira Islands; my father's family hailed from the Azores. My mother's family were laborers. My paternal grandfather was a blacksmith, and others on my father's side were also more into business. Both my father's family and my mother's family migrated to Hawaii. I'm still searching how and when.

My mother married my father on March 29, 1943. I had a sister who was stillborn in 1943. I was born on January 20, 1945. My father was previously married and he had two children.

My father handled all the books and financials for Liberty House, the largest, most prestigious department store in Hawaii at the time. The Neiman Marcus of Hawaii, Liberty House was "the" place to shop.

My father played shortstop on the amateur baseball team in Hawaii. He is featured in the book *Athletes of Hawaii*, plus I have a newspaper clipping stating that he went to St. Louis College in Hawaii and played for the Liberty House team.

We lived on Olokele Avenue in Honolulu. The street was a dead end and there was a park nearby where he would practice baseball and I would watch him at times. Everybody knew him.

My father played slack key on the steel guitar. My uncle Johnny, who ran a dairy, played the guitar, while my uncle Harold played the ukulele and my cousin and uncle Adolph played the accordion. Adolph was both my cousin and uncle because he was the son of my uncle, plus he married my mother's sister. (There was no blood relation between Adolph and my mother's sister.)

In Hawaii, you play music, sing or dance. Living on an island, you work and get together, and people in Hawaii love to have parties. There were often parties that lasted all weekend, with plenty of laughing, singing, and, yes, drinking. As children, we would play and fall asleep anywhere.

I remember Uncle Johnny's house in particular because he lived on Kamehameha Highway near the ocean and you could hear the waves. I loved that sound.

* * *

The more I learned about my father (which was not until many years later), the more I realized how much he and I had in common. He not only knew a lot of people, but had a generous spirit and a natural inclination for helping others, including helping his brother Johnny run his dairy by taking care of his books. Plus, as I mentioned, he made his living as an accountant.

As it happens, many years later, when I was in my twenties and raising my daughter as a single mother, I landed a job in the accounting department at ARC Specialties in Houston. For some reason, I have always had an affinity for accounting and bookkeeping. I never really understood why, until I discovered that my father was an accountant.

Then again, accounting is all about math, and math is all about numbers. With numbers, there is logic and order. If there's an error in the company ledger, there's usually a reason why. All you have to do is find it. So, when I think about all the challenges and disorder I faced throughout the first two decades of my life, I suppose, deep down, I found comfort and stability in the order that came from working with numbers all day.

My earliest memory of my father was going to St. Patrick's Catholic Church with him. He had a Model T Ford and I'd stand up in the seat next to him. I loved that church, especially the stained glass windows. I would stand on the seat at church next to my father and look at those windows.

Though I did not fully understand it at the time, those memories of going to church with my father proved to be one of God's saving graces. At the very least, it reminded me that, before my mother remarried, I once had a normal relationship with a loving, giving father. That's how I was able to gauge, even at so young an age, that what my stepfather was doing to me was abnormal and wrong.

* * *

I always felt undying love from my father, but I don't remember feeling that from my mother. I suppose that stems from how she was raised by her own mother.

By all accounts, my maternal grandmother, in her younger years, was not a great person. If my father had a personality that attracted people, my maternal grandmother made others recoil. Money and material things were important to her; people mattered only so long as she could get something out of them.

To say my grandmother was not a good mother is an understatement. She did not show love to her daughters because she saw them as a hindrance; not only that, she *could* not show love to her daughters, because she lacked that basic human capacity. She was extremely controlling and expected total allegiance of her children. What she said, you did—no matter what, and no matter how old you were. She had this tremendous hold on her children, especially with my mother.

My Aunty Alice was the oldest, my mother was the middle child, and my Aunty Rita was the youngest. Because Aunty Rita spent several years in a boarding school, she did not face some of the cruelties that my mother and Aunty Alice endured.

I'm sure my mother suffered as a result of her upbringing—in fact, I know she did. She was as emotionally detached to us as my grandmother was to her.

That may account for why, as vividly as I remember going to church with my birth father, I can't say the same for my mother. While I'm sure she also went with us, my memories of her in those early years are not nearly as clear as those I have of him.

My mother was also as much of a narcissist as my maternal grandmother. I say this not to bash her (for that's not what this book is about), but simply to show that we learn things from our parents, whether we realize it or not. The traits, behavior, and values that we observe as children leave an indelible mark on us, shaping the people that we eventually become as adults. In the case of my mother, the values she inherited from my grandmother will give you some understanding as to why she did not protect my siblings and me. But it also explains some other things.

I felt that my mother acted jealous of me, even when I was two years old. Strange as that may sound at first, it makes sense, given the context of her upbringing. Before I was born, my mother had been the apple of my father's eye. But that changed once I was born. Up until the day she died, she loved to tell stories about "how attractive she was." Like my maternal grandmother, she liked the attention.

When I was young, I had photos of my father's family and a little picture of my father in my dresser drawer—the same one that appears on his gravestone. One day, several years after he died, I went into my room and discovered that all of those pictures were gone. They were taken away so that I would no longer have any contact with my father or his family.

Looking back I believe my stepfather removed those pictures so that I would forget my father. Or perhaps my mother did.

The author at age two

CHAPTER TWO
The Grooming

My stepfather was career Navy from San Antonio, Texas. His mother, a Hispanic, was born in Nuevo Laredo, Texas, while his father was from a small town near Corpus Christi.

In Hawaii in those days, if you married a military man you were doing well.

Soon after my stepfather married my mother, he was transferred to California, which meant we were all going to California. We moved to Hayward, a city in Alameda County, Northern California, about an hour southeast of San Francisco. We lived in Hayward for the next four years.

My mother had two children with my stepfather. Both were girls. One half-sister, whom I'll call California, was born in 1950. The other, whom I'll call Vegas, was born the following year.

My maternal grandmother, as it happens, also lived in Hayward. My grandfather had died before I was born and she had since remarried and moved there. She and her second husband lived several miles away from us.

Our house was right across the street from Cherryland Elementary School, where I attended kindergarten through fourth grade. I loved school almost as much as I loved going to church. I had lots of friends in school, and if I could I would have spent all my time there.

We lived next door to a Portuguese family whose children received lessons in catechism from the nuns at All Saints Cathedral in Hayward. The nuns would go to our neighbors' house to teach classes. When my mother learned about this, she arranged for me to attend those classes along with our neighbors' children. Because of that, I was able to receive my first communion at All Saints Cathedral when I was seven or eight. (A few years later, after we had moved back to Hawaii, I received the sacrament of confirmation when I was twelve.)

Beyond the trappings of the Church, God has always been a part of my life—even at a young age. I always said my prayers. I always talked to Him. I'm sure I didn't say the kind of prayers that most people would say. I just talked to Him all the time, especially in those moments when my stepfather abused me. I didn't understand why this man was doing this to me, but I knew it didn't feel right. It comforted me to know that, when there was no one else that I could talk to, I could always turn to God.

That's why my faith has been such a vital part of my life. Somehow, especially during my young years, I always felt as though someone was guiding me whenever I needed it most. Either I would get a feeling or something would enter my mind to help me. Even as an adult I've had moments when I would experience intensely strong feelings—feelings that were so strong, I would be guided by them.

I have no idea why or where this comes from. All I know is that, whenever I get these feelings, I pay close attention.

* * *

During those four years in Northern California, several events took place. Though some of my memories are sketchy, others I remember explicitly. I can remember everything about my stepfather, but I have very little recollection about birthdays, holidays or any of the other things that most kids my age looked forward to celebrating.

One day, I was playing in my room when suddenly, I felt compelled to go in my closet where I had all my stuffed animals and make a place to hide in case my stepfather came looking for me. I got it all ready. I know I had to be about five years old because I remember I had just started kindergarten.

The next day, we were all outside working in the yard: my siblings, my mother, and my stepfather. In the back of our garage was the chicken coop where they raised rabbits and chickens. We had apple trees in the backyard and a little garden. The chicken coop was the place where I had that first encounter with my stepfather.

I had to go to the bathroom, so I went into the house. My bedroom had a door that went out to the back porch, catty-corner to another door that went into the house through the laundry room. I went in the house through my door, which was unlocked. I made sure I locked it when I went in.

I was in the bathroom when I heard the other door open leading into the laundry room in the house. I hurried into my room and hid in the closet space I'd prepared. I heard footsteps coming down the hall and stopping at my room. My heart was pounding, I was so scared. Then my closet door opened. I remained very still in my space under my stuffed animals until the footsteps went back to the outside door and out. Then I got out of my safe space. I looked through the window and I saw all my family out there. He was out there. I knew from the sound of his steps that it was my stepfather that had come in.

I went out the front door, around the side of the house and looked through the gate into the backyard. When I saw he wasn't there, I slipped through the gate and went back to work in the yard like everybody else. At some point, he saw me. I know he had to wonder just how on earth I had made it back outside without him spotting me. But he never said a word about it.

Because my stepfather was in the military, there were stretches when he would go off to sea for months at a time. In the Navy, they called it maneuvers. He was in and out of port. For me, these were times when I was at peace, because I knew he wasn't around.

Cherryland Elementary School,
which the author attended as a young girl
when she lived in Hayward, California

The house in Hayward where the author lived as a young girl

CHAPTER THREE
The Letters

Around 1955 my stepfather was transferred back to Hawaii. I was in fourth or fifth grade. We ended up in Aiea, where I attended Alvah A. Scott School. We lived in a house behind the sugarcane mill.

Upon returning to the Islands, the only members of my mom's family that we saw was my Aunty Rita, Uncle Adolph, and two cousins. We no longer had any contact with anyone from my father's family. I didn't realize this until many years later, but they were not allowed to talk to us. Around this time, anything associated with my father, including the photos in my room, began to disappear. It was as though he had never existed.

My stepfather's rank in the Navy was boatswain's mate. Every time he came back from maneuvers, he would invite some of the seamen who served under him to come by the house. He'd host these loud drinking parties that lasted until dawn (or until the last man passed out, whichever came first). I remember waking up in the morning and stepping over all of their sleeping bodies. That was a norm.

My mother's sister, Alice, came to live with us for a while. She slept in the bedroom shared by my half-sisters California and Vegas, while my sister, Jersey, and I slept in the room next to them. One time, I heard some noise in the middle of the night. Though I always kept my door closed, I opened it a crack and heard my stepfather talking to Aunty Alice. He was trying to get inside their room. She firmly told him no.

The next day, I overheard my Aunty Alice telling my mother what my stepfather tried to do. My mother refused to believe her. "You're lying," she kept saying.

When I heard my mother say that, my heart sank.

Though I was getting older, I had never talked to my mother about what my stepfather had done to me. If she didn't believe Aunty Alice, no way would she believe me.

* * *

My stepfather also tried to intimidate me. He spoke menacingly, making it very clear that the only way I could do anything, or go anywhere with my friends, was to "be nice to him."

That's one way in which child molesters groom their victims: Basically, they're saying do something for me—meaning, "Keep your mouth shut and let me get away with doing whatever sexual things I have in mind"—and I'll do something for you.

Much to my stepfather's dismay, I would not

cooperate. While I hadn't found the courage to tell my mother yet, I refused to "be nice to him." Consequently, whenever my stepfather was home from maneuvers, I was usually made to clean the house, as though I were on his ship, every nook and cranny.

Sometimes my stepfather did things that practically dared me to tell on him. One day, he told me, "Look under the clothes hamper in the bathroom. I left you something there. Read it and flush it down the toilet."

Of course, knowing what would happen if I didn't do as I was told, I went to the hamper and found a letter. I read it. I can't recall the exact words, but it contained vivid, sexually explicit language along the lines of "I want you." He made it clear that I was the object of his desire, and said it in a way that he hoped would provoke a response.

I was eleven years old at the time.

I told him I had destroyed the letter, but I lied. I kept it hidden in a tube-like box where I stored my hula instruments. It was the perfect hiding place. My mother and my stepfather would never think of looking inside there.

That was not the only graphic letter I received from my stepfather. As I recall he wrote about two dozen others, all of which I also hid. I knew from these letters that he was doing something wrong, and I wanted someone to see them. But I didn't know if there was anyone that I could trust enough to show them to.

In one letter he made a reference to "You Don't Know Me," the 1956 song by Eddy Arnold that was a big hit at the time. He said that song was an expression of "how he felt" about me. He even wrote down some of the lyrics:

No, you don't know the one
Who dreams of you at night
And longs to kiss your lips
And longs to hold you tight

To this day, whenever I hear this song, I can't help but think of those letters.

Not only that, but when my stepfather told me it was "his song" to me, it made me think that he had gone after me simply because I was not his daughter. It never dawned on me then that I was not the only target in our family.

* * *

One morning, after another of my stepfather's all-night parties after coming home from maneuvers, I came out of my bedroom in my robe and made my way to the kitchen. By this time, even as a young girl, I was drinking coffee. As a baby, I could never drink milk. It didn't agree with me. My mother then tried strawberry milk or chocolate milk, but I could barely tolerate those, either. Finally, she gave me coffee with a lot of milk in it, because coffee had a strong taste. I'd even use it in my cornflakes in place of milk.

I went to the kitchen and saw one of the seamen who had partied with my stepfather seated at the kitchen table. He had already made a pot of coffee, so I poured myself a cup and sat down at the table with him.

The seaman was really nice. He could not have been more than nineteen years old, maybe twenty. I can't remember his name. But, since I believe my stepfather's ship at the time, *USS Black*, was stationed at Pearl Harbor, let's call him "Seaman Black."

We made idle chitchat for a few minutes. Then he said to me, "Your father"—at which point I promptly told him that he was not my father, but my stepfather.

"Your stepfather is not a nice man," said Seaman Black.

"I know," I replied.

"You need to be very careful."

"I know," I said.

Years later I would discover that what happened to me was not uncommon among children in military families, particularly in the 1950s. Unfortunately, if a wife tried to inform anyone about incidents of abuse, she was met with radio silence. The military or state police would not intervene because it was considered a "private matter."

That is why I am so grateful to have met Seaman Black that morning. It was almost like a sign of providence—as if God was telling me, "No matter what happens, you are not alone. You will be OK."

We sat and talked for a while longer. Then he said, "I have to shove off soon and go back to the mainland." (At the time, Hawaii was still a U.S. territory, not a state. That's why they called the continental U.S. the mainland.)

"When I get home, I'm going to send you something," he promised.

Eventually, I received a package from him. I think he may have been Catholic, because it contained a crucifix. The crucifix was actually a portable altar that slides up to stand on a base. The stand has two places for very small candles and a small vial of holy water.

I never saw or heard from Seaman Black again, but I have that cross to this day, and it's still very important to me.

Sometimes I wish I could remember his actual name, so that I can look him up and let him know how much I appreciate what he did for me. You never know how a kindness toward a child can be a lifeline.

* * *

I spent a lot of time at St. Elizabeth's Catholic Church. It was several miles away, and the only way I could get there was by walking. But that didn't matter to me. School and church were always my two sanctuaries.

Sometimes when my stepfather was away on maneuvers, we'd visit my aunt and uncle at their house in Kokohead. There, my uncle Johnny owned a dairy, which his son Adolph ran. I spent time with my cousin Laverne. We'd go out and watch them milk the cows, then we'd run and play on the haystacks. Those were all good memories. We were free to run and play without thinking about or worrying about anything.

During this time my maternal grandmother, Ida, came to visit from California. She slept in the same room with me. I thought to myself, "This is it. I'm going to show these letters to my grandmother and when she tells my mother, she will have to believe me."

One night, when we were all lying in bed, I pulled all of the letters out and showed them to my grandmother. She read them. Then she looked at me and said, "I'll deal with these."

The next day, my grandmother told my mother about the letters. In trying to explain his reprehensible actions my mother came up with a story about how my stepfather "had a plate in his head, from when he served in World War II."

Granted, many soldiers came home from World War II and Korea with battle scars: physical, psychological and emotional. Many exhibited symptoms of what we now call post-traumatic stress disorder by lashing out at their loved ones. While that does not in any way excuse their behavior, it may account for the higher than average percentage of abuse in military families.

The trouble with that explanation is that my stepfather never served in World War II. He joined the Navy in 1949, four years after the war ended, and just around the time when he first met my mother. Nor did he see any battle in Korea.

Not only that, but many years later, when I was an adult, I told the story about "the plate in his head" to my stepfather's sister. According to his sister, my stepfather was never injured in all the years he served in the Navy. He didn't even have any scars. (And besides, we know my stepfather was already a predator by the time he met my mother. Remember what he tried to do to me at that party at my aunt's house.)

Now you may ask why would my mother even think of such a story? Well, part of that answer stems from her own deep-seated narcissism. As many experts will tell you, narcissists have an elastic relationship with the truth: They will lie without compunction, especially when they feel threatened or cornered.

Beyond that, however, my mother had other reasons for defending that man. We will get to all of that later.

After a long talk, my grandmother said that she wanted to take me back to California with her. I wanted to go, but my mother refused. Then my grandmother left without me.

I was terrified. I had "told" on my stepfather. It was only a matter of time before my mother confronted him about those letters. I would have to face the wrath of that terrible man.

Oddly enough (or perhaps not so odd, given her narcissism), my mother was more upset over what he "had done to her" than what he had done to me. Still, she told me that everything was fine and that my stepfather "wasn't going to do that anymore."

But it wasn't fine. Instead, my stepfather looked for other ways to make my life a "living hell." Every time he thought something needed cleaning in that house, from scrubbing the baseboards to the toilets, that became my job. It was if I had been transformed into a real-life Cinderella.

The house in Aiea, Hawaii, where the author lived circa 1955

The cross that Seaman Black gave to the author

View of Pearl Harbor from Aiea, Hawaii

CHAPTER FOUR
Getting Braver and Stronger

Time went on. My stepfather would be gone and back again. The quality of my life always improved whenever he was away.

In 1958, when I was in seventh grade, there was a huge rock 'n' roll contest in Hawaii. Of course, rock 'n' roll was *the* biggest thing, while music was another refuge for me.

I loved music. I knew every song that was out. I lived for church, school, and music.

The contest was hosted by Tom Moffatt, the Dick Clark of Honolulu. Originally from Michigan, he was a popular radio DJ and concert promoter who brought many of the biggest names in music to the Islands, including Elvis Presley, Chuck Berry, Frank Sinatra and, later, The Rolling Stones, The Doors and Michael Jackson.

This particular contest was for kids eighteen and under from all over the island. Anyone could enter. My girlfriend Myra, who had become my best friend in Hawaii since my family moved back there a few years earlier, wanted me to go with her. When I was not home, I was with Myra.

My stepfather was in town at that time and I knew he would never allow it. But I was almost a teenager then, and as I grew older, I became braver. I no longer cared about the consequences. I was going to that contest. I told Myra that I was going to sneak out of the house. She said she would meet me.

The contest was held in the Aiea Gym in Aiea, which was the place that all the kids went to go swimming, play volleyball, etc. We sat in the bleachers on the floor of the gym, along with all of the other kids. Many of them were out on the floor, dancing to music. Tom Moffatt was also among them, looking for the best dancers.

One boy, Larry Cordero, asked my friend Yvonne to dance. She didn't want to. He asked another girl. Same answer. Finally, somebody suggested that I dance with Larry, so I did.

I didn't even know Larry Cordero and had never danced with him before. But since I went there to dance in the first place, I figured it couldn't hurt. Wouldn't you know, we were picked as one of the ten couples who were finalists.

The couples danced one at a time to different songs. Larry and I danced to "Rock Around the Clock," and he did some fancy moves like putting his leg over me and pulling me through his legs and up in the air and down. I was able to follow him because I loved to dance.

Finally, all of the couples lined up and Tom Moffatt stood behind each one. The audience voted by clapping hands, cheering and yelling.

We were the youngest couple and, in the end, we won that contest! They presented us with a trophy. For a moment I was on top of the world, like Cinderella on the night of the ball—but then reality set in. "I can't tell anybody that I won," I thought. "I'm not even supposed to be here. I'm going to be in a lot of trouble."

Making matters worse, at that moment Myra came over and whispered, "Your stepfather is here."

I looked up and, sure enough, I saw him. "Well, that's it," I thought. "I'm dead now."

Yet, to my surprise, my stepfather wasn't angry at all. Sure, he made me go home right away, but now he could brag to all the men on his ship that his stepdaughter had won this big rock 'n' roll contest.

Plus, because Tom Moffatt also hosted a popular TV dance show in Hawaii that was the equivalent of *American Bandstand*, one of the prerequisites of winning the contest was that Larry and I had to appear on Moffatt's show before we could collect any other prizes. My mother let me go on that show, and my stepfather got to boast about that, too. I suppose that made him feel like a bigger man than he actually was.

Still, I wonder: How on earth did he know I wasn't in my bed that night? He must have gone to my room and pulled the covers back. So much for "assuring" my mother that he "would never do that again."

Sometime later, long after the contest, my mother informed me that she had to throw the trophy away because it had been broken. But she kept the plaque and gave it to me. My mother never explained what happened to the trophy, but I wonder whether my stepfather had something to do with it.

* * *

In the summer of 1959, just before Hawaii became a state, we transferred back to Northern California. I had just finished the eighth grade and was about to start my freshman year in high school.

One day, a few weeks before we left Hawaii, I happened to look out the front door and see my stepfather talking to my sister, Jersey. She stood frozen, like a rabbit caught in the crosshairs, as he peered intently at her.

Suddenly I realized I was not his only target. He had gone after Jersey as well.

When she went back inside the house, I asked Jersey, "Is he saying or doing anything bad to you? You have to tell me if he is. You have to tell me."

Initially, Jersey denied it. But later she opened up to me. "Yes," she said quietly. "He's been touching me."

Now it made sense. He had targeted my sister and me because we were not his children. I was not aware at that time that he was abusing my half-sisters—his own two daughters—as well. He had hidden that well.

A few weeks later, after we had boarded the military personnel transport ship en route to California, I told Jersey to make sure that she was never alone on the ship. "Whatever you do, you need to stay with me at all times," I said. "When we get to California, I'll talk to Mom and tell her that she has to do something."

In my heart, I really believed that she would

finally protect us. I could not have been more wrong.

The journey back to the Golden State was not fun because I was seasick for the entire five days. When we finally docked, we moved back into the same house where we had previously lived, across the street from the elementary school.

Fortunately, shortly after we arrived, my stepfather left again for a period of time. That gave us time to get situated in school. That also gave me time to confront my mother.

"You have to do something," I remember telling her. "You need to protect us."

She was nervous and upset. "Don't worry," she kept saying. "I'll take care of it."

I can't tell you how many times I heard her say that.

I kept hounding her, but eventually I realized she would never help us. It would be several years before I finally learned the reason why.

* * *

When I was a freshman in high school, I had a boyfriend, Wayne, that I really liked and felt safe with. I say "boyfriend," but it was really very innocent—I could never go to dances, or football games, or the prom, or any other school activity or equivalent of a "real" date because I refused to "be nice" to my stepfather.

I may not have had a social life in high school, but I continued to grow stronger. I hated my stepfather. While he wasn't bothering me as much at this point, he was always trying *something*.

In hindsight, I think my stepfather was the type of creep who went after little girls. As I became older, and he found that I wasn't going to be "receptive," he simply moved down the line of victims.

One day, while sitting at the kitchen table, I finally decided that I would no longer look at this man. I wasn't going to talk to him. I wouldn't give him the time of day. Instead, I completely ignored him.

Being a narcissist, my stepfather couldn't stand that. It made him angry.

One night after dinner, while my mother was taking a bath, Jersey and I were in the kitchen. I was washing dishes and she was drying them. I had to have been about sixteen. My stepfather came over to me and whispered in my ear: "You bitch."

I was cleaning a pan and my hands were full of soapsuds. Instinctively I turned around and flung the pan at him. He stepped back, and it crashed into the wall.

For a moment I was afraid he might hit me—until I saw the fear in his eyes and shock on his face. It was the same look of terror I had seen in Jersey when he towered over her that day in Hawaii. Suddenly I realized he was nothing but a bully. Once he saw that I had some power, he became afraid of me.

My mother heard the commotion and rushed out. "What's going on?" she asked.

"Ask him," I said. I saw no point in saying anything else because she wasn't going to do anything anyway.

A day or so later, my mother came to me and

said, "You have to leave."

I said, "Leave and go where?"

"I don't care," she replied. "He doesn't want you here anymore."

Now there was no doubt: I would never get any support from that woman. Not against him. What kind of mother does this?

She called my grandmother. I ended up living with her and my step-grandfather at their house in Hayward.

Being so young and naïve, I figured that I still had my boyfriend. All I had to do was finish school, marry my boyfriend and then all my siblings could come and live with me.

I know it sounds illogical now, but in my mind at the time I thought it was a good plan. I was clueless and isolated.

* * *

When you go through something like this, people are quick to say, "Well, you should have done this, you should have done that."

They're wrong. I couldn't do anything because my mother would not support me. Where would I go and get help? Would we be taken away and protected?

Sometimes the fear of the unknown—where will I go, what will become of me—is worse than the abuse.

Even though they may be sexually or physically abused, young children know their home situation. They don't want to go somewhere they don't know. They're afraid.

My brother was never sexually abused by my

stepfather, but he endured other cruelties. If he did something "stupid" (like kids are prone to do), my mother would tell my stepfather. He would go out to my brother's room, which was outside attached to the garage where we lived in California, and beat my brother with a strap.

I hated my mother for that.

What purpose did it serve to tell my stepfather? My brother was not a delinquent. She knew that. She also knew what kind of man my stepfather was. Yet she did nothing to protect her children.

I know my story can't be the only one like this in the world.

Plaque that the author received for winning the dance contest

Sunset High School in Hayward, California,
which the author attended as a freshman in 1959

CHAPTER FIVE
Looking Back

When I was a child in Hawaii, people never locked their doors or did anything like that. You could go out and play all day, or camp on the beaches, and no one ever worried. You had much more freedom then.

The beauty of Hawaii was the land and landscape. Oh, there's still beauty, mind you, but some of the mystique has been taken away by all of the buildings and highways. It's just very different now. Not the same at all.

I mentioned that we returned to California in 1959, shortly before Hawaii became our fiftieth state. Some people on the islands were happy about that development—they thought it was a wonderful thing. Others, not so much. Some natives, in fact, fervently wish for Hawaii not to be a state again. But there's no way that could ever happen.

There were not as many white (haole) people in Hawaii when I grew up there. If you were white, you stood out. Same if you were a military kid. The government had special schools for children in military families. If they lived off the base, they might go to schools such as Radford High School in Honolulu, where I went to school. Radford was close to the base at Pearl Harbor and had a lot of military kids, whom I met and liked. (Prior to Radford, though, I went to Aiea High School on the island of Oahu.)

Traffic today is a nightmare. When I was a child, my cousin/uncle Adolph, along with his wife, managed my uncle Johnny's dairy farm on the southeast side of the island. We'd go over there and visit them periodically. Back then, the only way to get to the other side of the island was a really far drive up over the Pali—a steep, treacherous hill that wound around the mountain. There were no barriers on either side of the Pali, while the road was so narrow there was barely enough room for two cars to pass. If you got too far over, you could fall off the mountain.

As a kid, I was always petrified to go over the Pali. I could never look out the window—instead, I would hide on the floorboards of Adolph's woody station wagon. It was that scary.

The very top of the Pali was the windiest point on the island. As you approached it, you always had to roll down your windows so that the wind could blow through the car. Otherwise, it might blow you against the mountain. (Once you got past that point, it was okay to roll them back.)

The Pali is still the windiest point on Hawaii, but the roadway is closed off now. Too many accidents occurred on that road, and far too many deaths. After Hawaii became a state, they built the Wilson Tunnel through the Pali, though many people today still hike down that Pali road. There's even a lookout up there.

* * *

There's always an island breeze in Hawaii. No matter how warm it is during the day, it's going to be cool at night—and in the wintertime, it can be *really* cool.

Then again, in Hawaii, if the temperature drops to 60 degrees at night, people think it's freezing. They'll start putting on their warmups and other heavy clothes.

The rainy season is February and March, when it rains more than normal (and often in unusual ways). On the island, it can rain on one side of the street, but not on the other. Sometimes it even rains when the sun is still out. We call that Liquid Sunshine.

Hawaii is a paradise for the terrain, the beauty, and the flowers. All of the plants are a sight to behold. Even today with all the build-up, you can find the beauty in Hawaii. If you're from there, it's in your heart.

I love going back and seeing everyone again, but I wouldn't want to live there again—especially on Oahu. It's become too crowded and very expensive. The other islands are not quite as crowded, though it won't be long before they get that way.

It amazes me how all of the different flowers in Hawaii each have their own distinct aroma, whether it's the crown flower or the pikake. The plumeria, the plant from which the common lei garlands are made, is especially fragrant. I especially like the ginger flowers that grow wild. They smell extremely strong.

If you pick them and put them in your house, the scent of ginger will pervade.

Contrast that with the flowers in California. Some of them have no smell at all. I remember how shocked I was when I first discovered that. I could not imagine flowers not smelling sweet, since it was predominant in Hawaii.

There are plenty of varieties of fruit in Hawaii, including mangos (the most common fruit), guavas, mountain apples, lilikoi and, of course, pineapple. There are also a lot of what Hawaiians call "pear trees." (In the continental United States, they are known as avocados, but avocados are actually from the pear family.) To this day, I still associate pears with avocados, because on the islands we didn't have the particular fruit that is commonly known as pears.

Other trees in Hawaii include Banyan trees, which can live for hundreds of years, and kiawe trees, a species of mesquite. I didn't know that about kiawes until years later, when my Hawaiian friend Myra came to visit me on the mainland and marveled at all the mesquite trees. Only she kept calling them kiawe trees.

* * *

When I was really young, I didn't have a lot of toys. Nor do I remember anything about Christmas, birthday celebrations, or any of the other kinds of things that children normally enjoy and look forward to. I do remember having a doll that I liked, though. I also remember riding my bike, because that gave me a sense of freedom.

I didn't play with my siblings very much since

they were much younger than me. Sometimes I would take my brother with me when I rode my bike, and we'd play hide and seek. As I got older, I was always the one who had to babysit them. I was put in charge of them so much, it was as if I were their mother.

My brother and my sisters would always say, "You're not the boss of me." I didn't choose to be the boss; I was made to be the boss.

I told you that music, school, and church were all sanctuaries for me. I remember *everything* about school: my teachers, my classes, and all that we learned. I hated it when vacation time came around. I wanted to go to school all year.

We were living in California when I started kindergarten, and we stayed there until the beginning of fourth grade. When I was in first and second grade, my teacher both years was Mrs. Fosman. My third-grade teacher was Mrs. Casey, while my fourth-grade teacher was Mrs. Monroe. We had all the same kids in the first, second, and third grade. They were like a separate family.

We did so many fun things in school. At that time, we learned ballroom dancing with boys and girls and we learned the foxtrot, the tango, and many other dances. It amazes me that they taught us things like that—but they did. Learning how to dance together, especially at that young an age, teaches boys and girls how to interact with each other, in a positive way. It's also a lot of fun.

I also remember learning multiplication in third grade. They would tell us $2x2=4$ and have us memorize that. At first, I didn't understand: How could two times two equal four just by saying that?

Then a little boy, Art Martin, showed me by drawing two little sticks on paper and had me count them. Then he drew another two sticks and we added them all up. A-ha! Then he showed me 2x3 and by drawing two sets of three sticks and adding those up. That was how I learned multiplication. Once I understood how to figure it out in my mind, then I could memorize it.

That may have been another early sign of my interest in accounting and bookkeeping. When you get down to it, accounting is figuring out problems in your head and then putting it on paper.

Creative subjects, such as art, were among my favorites in elementary school. I especially loved penmanship—first learning how to write in print, then learning how to write in script. I thought they were both very artistic.

When I was eight, going on nine, we moved back to Hawaii, where I attended school from fifth grade through eighth grade. For some reason, the education in Hawaii was not nearly as good as in California. I don't know what the difference was, but my teachers in California seemed more dedicated.

In Hawaii, my sixth-grade teacher was Mr. Dutchman. I did not like him. He was awful. He was mean. He was a horrible teacher. The less said about him, the better.

This brings us up to 1959, when we were transferred back to California. Beginning with ninth grade, I attended high school in California until I left there, in my junior year.

My history teacher in high school was Mr. Flesuras. He was excellent. I thought for sure I would hate history, because I didn't want to memorize dates.

But he made every class so interesting because he taught it by telling a story.

Mr. Flesuras was also our guidance counselor. At the start of my freshman year, he told me I had to take algebra. That made me nervous: Algebra seemed so foreign to me, compared to normal math. But he kept telling me that I could do it—and what do you know, I passed.

My sophomore year, Mr. Flesuras wanted me to take geometry. I certainly didn't want to do that. I didn't like all of those squares and triangles. But he said, "If you don't like it, I'll move you." After a few weeks, he did.

Finally, he put me in bookkeeping. That's where I really excelled. In high school, business was my passion: bookkeeping, shorthand, typing, business English, and business math.

* * *

I remember both of the houses where I grew up vividly, partly because I had to clean them. But I also remember all of the places where I escaped and hid from my stepfather.

Our house in California was a two-bedroom with a master bedroom (with its own bath), kitchen/dining area, and living room. My half-sisters slept in a bedroom down the hall, across from the other bathroom. Next-door to their bedroom was the room I shared with Jersey. (That was the room with the door to the outside, which I told you about earlier.) My brother slept in a room next to the detached double car garage.

The house in Hawaii was much smaller. It had a

living room and a small dining room that had a bed up against the wall. That was where my brother slept. The kitchen area had a little table and chairs. Down the hall to the left was the master bedroom and a bathroom in the hallway. My half-sisters slept in one room at the end of the hall, while I shared a room with Jersey.

The house in Hawaii was made of wood. The one in California was stucco.

As I say, I did a lot of cleaning and washing. Eventually, I became interested in cooking, but I never told my mother that (otherwise, I'd end up with that job, too). I watched and knew how to cook. I just didn't do it.

Hula lessons were another thing that I loved and enjoyed doing. I did well and performed in many different parades, along with our halau. (A halau is hula school or troop that, in some ways, is like a family.) When you belonged to a halau, you not only earn a certificate at the end stating that you were trained as a dancer, but are given a special Hawaiian name.

My Hawaiian name is Lei Aloha, which means "a lei of love." Aloha means many things in Hawaii, including hello, love, and goodbye.

* * *

As a Catholic when you have children, you are obligated to raise them as Catholics. You must be sure they learn their catechism and receive the sacraments of communion and confirmation.

Of the seven sacraments in the Catholic Church, communion is the most important. Therefore, one's first holy communion is a big deal. As a child, I was going to accept Christ in my body. Take him in. The boys were dressed in little suits, while the girls were dressed in white—white dress, white shoes, and a little white veil—as if you were a little bride.

When you receive communion you were taught not to chew it, but let it dissolve in your mouth. Everybody was excited. It was a very special day.

I know my brother went through the communion ceremony. I think Jersey did, too. (As for my half-sisters, I don't remember.)

We never knew my stepfather's family until much later in life. Sometime after we returned to California, they decided to do a road trip to San Antonio. I think I was fifteen. That was the first time I ever saw any of them. For that matter, that was the first time *any* of us saw them.

I remember thinking how they were different from him. Of course, I never said anything like that— you just couldn't, because of what would happen if you did.

That's the thing that most people don't understand about victims of sexual abuse: You're afraid to come forward and talk about it for fear of retaliation.

This was especially true in the case of my siblings and me. It was not as if we had a protector who could take us away from it all. It was very isolating.

You know how most families have friends and neighbors with children, and they all get together and know one another? We didn't do that. We were not allowed to communicate with anyone outside the family, even when my stepfather was gone.

When I look back, I think my mother wanted it to be that way so that no one knew anything. Another control mechanism.

CHAPTER SIX
A Harsh Lesson About Justice

I went to live with my grandparents in Hayward in January 1962, just before I turned seventeen. I remember celebrating my birthday there. I lived with them maybe three months at the most.

One day I came home from school to find my grandmother really upset. "A lady came to the house," she said. "She wants to talk to you."

"Who is she?" I asked.

"I don't know," said my grandmother. "But she is coming back this afternoon."

Sometime later, the woman came to the door and said that she had a car waiting outside. "I need to take you with me," she explained. "I need to talk to you."

That made my grandmother nervous. She didn't want me to go.

"It's OK," the woman assured her. "I'll bring her back."

She took me outside and walked me to the car. Jersey, Vegas, and California were all seated in the backseat. Suddenly I realized I was in a police car.

I asked my sisters what had happened. They told me they didn't know.

The woman drove us to a police station, took me into her office and started asking questions. She interviewed us each individually. As soon as she started asking about my stepfather, I knew something had happened.

The woman's office had a large glass window, out of which you could see all the goings-on of the rest of the station. At one point, I looked up and noticed some officers bringing my stepfather in. He was wearing handcuffs.

I remember how relieved I felt. Finally, I thought, the truth is going to come out.

* * *

I'm still not sure how everything transpired, but it involved one of my half-sisters. I don't know if she told a friend, and the friend told her mom, and the mom called the principal at their school. But somehow the police found out. They picked up Vegas, Jersey, and California at school before they came to get me.

That was the first time that I realized my stepfather had also victimized his own daughters.

The woman began her interview with me by saying there had been a "report."

"Yes," I said. "He is a molester." I gave her all the information she wanted.

Then my mother walked in. She stood there looking at me, firmly believing that I had turned him in. "What have you done?" she finally said.

"I haven't done anything!" I yelled back.

The woman spoke firmly to my mother and tried to calm her down. "Your daughter didn't do anything," she told my mother. Then she asked her to take a seat.

The rest of the conversation remains a blur to me. The only thing I remember was that my sisters and I were placed under protective custody and taken to Snedigar Cottage in Hayward, which was the foster care section of the Alameda County Juvenile Hall. There, foster children, mostly age thirteen and under, lived while waiting to be placed in foster homes.

I also remember how hungry we were. We had been at the police station for hours with no food and nothing to drink. By the time we arrived at Snedigar, it was late at night and they gave us nothing to eat.

They told us that we would have to stay on different levels, in different areas. We had to get rid of our clothes and wear whatever they gave us. My siblings were so scared and upset—they did not want to be separated. But the staff said that they could not let us stay together because of our different ages.

We stayed at Snedigar for about three or four months. It felt like a prison.

* * *

We then had to attend a hearing. They sent us individually into a room and told us to tell our story. There was an audience and a panel of people seated in front of us that included my stepfather, my mother, and a man who I assume was my stepfather's lawyer. As I recall, there may have a few other people there who were representing our interests.

I told my siblings, "You have to tell everything. You have to tell them what happened." I made them promise. They said that they would.

They called us up one by one until finally it was my turn to speak. My stepfather's attorney started firing questions at me as if he were Perry Mason.

"Isn't it true that you don't like your stepfather?"

"Yes, that was true," I said.

"And isn't it true that you have made all of this up and you convinced your siblings to go along with this because you don't like him?

I could not believe what I was hearing. I had not done anything wrong—*he had*. Clearly, they were lying and creating this storyline: I was the bad one. I was the one who had coerced my siblings into saying these terrible things about my stepfather.

It made me wonder what would have happened if I had spoken up when I was younger. For all I know, my mother and stepfather would have put me in juvenile hall as an incorrigible child. Guilty until proven innocent.

I did everything I could do to compose myself. "Absolutely not," I said.

My mother sat right next to my stepfather, showing him support while acting as if nothing had happened. I never felt so alone.

Sometime later, I learned that my grandparents had put up the money for my mother to hire this lawyer to defend my stepfather, provided that I would go back to live with my grandparents afterward. That didn't happen.

* * *

After the hearing, there was a trial—and yet another shocking development. I was not allowed to testify; only my siblings were. But because they were so young and frightened, by the time they took the witness stand all they did was sit and cry. Each and every one of them was too traumatized to speak.

Again, I was beside myself: Why I was not allowed to testify? How does a legal system make that decision? Where were my rights? I was seventeen years old, one year away from being a legal adult in California. Why on earth did they feel I was not credible, just because my mother and stepfather said so?

That predator had victimized me since I was five years old—and now that I was older and stronger, and no longer as afraid of him as I once was, *I was not allowed to tell the court what he had done to me*?

Where was my mother's allegiance? Certainly not with her children.

Children who have been abused are usually too afraid to speak up until they become older and gain confidence—not just in themselves, but that someone will finally help them and believe them.

I thought the legal system was going to help us. It did not. The court should have put him in jail. It did not. It was all beyond my comprehension at the time.

All I knew was that we were innocent and he was guilty. What I did not realize is that, under the law, he was presumed innocent until proven guilty.

Cases such as ours are rarely resolved in favor of the children because of the nature of our legal system. We like to think it's about seeking justice, but it's really about which side has the better lawyer that can manipulate the law.

My stepfather and mother hired a lawyer who twisted the facts around. All I could do was seethe and feel more alone than ever.

Sadly, in most cases like ours, the children get lost in the shuffle. From the point of view of the victims, it appears as if no one cares what happens to them or what will happen to them in the future.

CHAPTER SEVEN
Moving to Texas

The end of the trial was devastating: My stepfather was acquitted. He was not going to jail. The court, however, ruled that Jersey, Vegas, California and I were to be taken away from my parents for one year. We ended up going back to Snedigar Cottage under protective custody until we left.

To this day, I have no idea if my siblings even understand the role my mother played in all of this. I think they looked at her like another victim. She certainly was not.

Over and over I approached my mother about my stepfather, to no avail. As I look back, it's clear to me that she had protected him—and, by doing so, colluded with him in his abuse of my sisters and me—by looking the other way.

Even more insidious, my mother eventually poisoned my own sister against me, though I did not know that at the time.

Remember, when I was sixteen years old and no longer afraid to stand up to my stepfather, my mother told me, "You can't live here anymore. He doesn't want you here." In other words, she threw me out. But that wasn't what she told Jersey. As I learned many years later from my half-sister Vegas, she convinced my sister and the rest of my siblings that I had "abandoned" them.

Now some of you may ask, "What about your brother, Dallas?" For some reason, the police did not pick him up that day when they took my sisters and me to the station. To be honest, I never learned what happened to him until many, many years later. He ran away because he was so distraught that we were all gone. Apparently, the police put out an alert and found him. They took him to juvenile hall because he was a runaway.

Years later, when I finally reconnected with Dallas, I learned that my mother had also misled him about me. We'll get to that story later.

* * *

Originally, the court had ruled that my sisters and I were supposed to stay at Snedigar until we moved in with family or were placed in foster care. One day, two or three months after the ruling, my mother arrived, along with another woman, and told us we were headed for the airport.

"Where are we going?" I asked.

My mother said, "San Antonio."

Apparently, the court said that, unless we were moved further than 100 miles from my parents, we would all go into foster care.

My grandparents lived too close to my mother, so I could not go back to them. Nor was Hawaii an option. None of my family over there knew anything about this—my mother and stepfather had seen to that because they didn't want anything discovered. Surely, if anyone in my family in Hawaii knew what had happened, they would have taken custody of us.

I have been hard on my mother, and rightfully so. But I will give her credit for this: She did not want us to be separated in foster care, so she made other arrangements. Looking back, it's probably the only thing in her life she ever did to help us.

As we boarded the plane to San Antonio, I had no idea where we were going. Then I found out that we would be living with my stepfather's mother. (For purposes of this story, we will call her Maria.) There could not have been a worse place to go.

This woman, Maria, had no love for my sister or me. Vegas and California, she did not mind because they were her biological granddaughters. But Jersey and I were another story. She saw us both as a big imposition.

For that matter, none of us wanted to be there, either. Maria's house was very small, and we were crowded together to sleep. I hated being there. While it was better than living with my mother and stepfather (and having to deal with him), overall it was another place that we did not want to be.

Again, I have to ask: Where was the court system? No one ever bothered to check on us. Once we were out of California, we were on our own.

* * *

We arrived in San Antonio in time to register for school. My mother stayed for a while and helped us get settled before returning to California.

I was seventeen years old and about to start my senior year of high school. I had no friends, I knew absolutely no one. That was hard enough. Then I found out that I couldn't take courses in any of the things that I had majored in when we were in California (like business). In Texas, you were required to take home economics. Learn to sew, learn to cook. I didn't want to take any of those courses, but I had to.

I muddled through school, made a few friends, and tried to figure out how to live. I didn't bother asking Maria's permission to go anywhere. I just told her what I was going to do and, besides, I don't think she particularly cared.

Maria had a full-time job. Every morning she always left for work first, then we went to school later. One day, I wasn't feeling well, so I stayed home from school. Knowing how much she resented me, I started poking around to see what, if anything, I might find that could tell me why we were sent to live there.

I came across a letter written by my mother and stepfather that basically rehashed all of the lies they had told the courts. In other words, I was the one who had lied about my stepfather and coerced all of my siblings into going along with it. He was totally innocent of any wrongdoing. I could not believe what I was reading.

No wonder Maria hated me. Here I was, this horrible person who had lied about her son, living in her house.

Later that morning, Maria's daughter (my stepfather's sister, whom we will call Lola), came by the house. Apparently, the school had contacted Maria, and she called Lola to check up on me.

"Why aren't you in school?" Lola asked.

"I wasn't feeling well," I said.

Then she said, "Why were you sent here?"

"What did they tell you?" I asked.

"We really don't know much of anything," she admitted. "Nothing they've told us has made any sense."

I told her everything.

I don't know if Lola believed me at the time—in fact, for many years I wasn't sure. Then one day, about thirty-five years later, we were on the phone with each other when she made a remark that changed everything. (While Lola and I were never close friends, we did stay in touch over the years.) During this conversation, she told me that her brother—my stepfather—was still alive with two sons and a daughter from another marriage. Apparently, my stepfather's daughter from this marriage was very belligerent to him.

Knowing what I knew about my stepfather, his daughter's behavior had to stem from him. The fruit, as they say, does not fall far from the tree.

But Lola was beside herself. "I don't understand why she treats him so callously," she said, "or why he allows her to speak to him that way."

"Why do you think she's so bad?" I asked.

She had no response.

At that point, it hit me: Lola had never believed a single word of what I had said about her brother.

Even after all these years.

Before too long the phone call ended. I never spoke to Lola again.

At first, I thought that, like her mother, she was simply in denial. But it's also possible that she never believed what had really happened.

Nevertheless, even if Lola did not believe me that day in 1962, she did reach out to me. "Maybe it would be better if you came to live at my house," she said.

So I went to live with Lola and her family, and my siblings stayed with Maria. I suppose you can consider that an act of providence because she delivered me from a bad situation.

Still, I was nearly eighteen years old and had much to learn about life. I was also carrying a lifetime of physical and emotional stress that was about to take its toll.

CHAPTER EIGHT
Ulcer

During my senior year, some friends introduced me to a guy in the Air Force. He soon became my boyfriend. He was a couple of years older than me. I had no clue about relationships. I had no clue about anything. My mindset was about the same as when I had my boyfriend in California. In other words, "If you are attracted to someone, you must be in love."

I was so naïve.

Now that I had a boyfriend, I also thought, "Maybe I'll marry this guy and take care of my siblings." If only life were that simple.

Graduation and my senior year meant nothing to me. I never went to a prom in my life. Graduation itself was little more than a certificate. I didn't feel the way about it that "normal" kids do.

Then again, up to that point, nothing in my life was remotely normal.

Just before graduation, the Air Force transferred

my boyfriend to Pakistan for two years. (So much for getting married.) I had no idea what to do or how I would live. Then that summer, shortly after I graduated, I met a guy named Phil. He lived at his sister's house, down the street. He had been in the Navy for a couple of years and got out with a medical discharge.

Meanwhile, I got a job as a secretary in a company in San Antonio. One of the girls needed another roommate for the house she shared. She asked me to live with her.

I told her, "I don't own anything." Which was true. I didn't have a car. I didn't have anything except my clothes.

"That's OK," she said. "You don't need anything. We have sheets and towels and pots and pans." So I moved in soon after I was hired.

I lived there with three other girls. It was one of those old wood-frame houses with a huge front porch, located in an old neighborhood, on a great street. (I believe it was on Mistletoe Avenue.) I thought it was a great arrangement—in fact, up to that point, it was the best thing that had ever happened in my life. I was working and making money. I took the bus to work. I took my clothes down to the washateria. This was 1963. You could do that back then.

Life was wonderful from the summer through October. Then two of the girls decided to move back home. That left two of us and we could not pay the rent for this house.

Once again I didn't know what to do. I had no place to go, and I certainly had no family.

Meanwhile, Phil and I had been seeing each

other. By this point, he had moved to an apartment not far from where I lived. When I told him that my roommates were moving, we decided to get married.

Why not?

Bear in mind, this had nothing to do with undying love or anything like that. My experience with boys was so limited, I didn't know the difference between love and attraction. I was fumbling through life, doing the best I could to survive. If anything, this decision came down to economics. We figured that it would be a lot cheaper if we lived together as one.

Phil and I were married on December 7, Pearl Harbor Day. Two weeks prior to that, John F. Kennedy was killed in Dallas.

Had I known then what I know now, I would have recognized both as omens.

* * *

When I married Phil, the only thing I really knew about him was that he seemed like a pretty nice guy.

A few weeks after we were married, I started feeling very ill. Given everything that I had gone through in my life to that point, I'm sure it was my nerves. I went to a doctor and he gave me pills that I had to take before and after meals. They didn't help.

One evening we were at Phil's mother's house. I was standing there watching her cook when I told her that I wasn't sure if I could eat. I drank a Diet Rite Cola and nibbled at my dinner.

By the time we returned to our apartment, I was so nauseated, I went to the bathroom and threw up. Everything was brown. I thought it was the cola. I went to bed, but thirty minutes later, I was back in the bathroom. Laid back down. Thirty minutes later, same thing—only this time, when I got out of bed and stood up, I was so disoriented that I could not walk. My equilibrium was off. I kept hitting the frame of the doorway.

Finally, I yelled for Phil. He helped me back to the bed and put a trash can beside it. I threw up all during the night.

The next morning, I was so weak, I could not get up. I could barely breathe. I felt as though I'd been punched so hard in the stomach, all the wind had been knocked out of me.

Phil took me to the emergency room at the hospital. They examined me and soon determined that I had lost 25 percent of my blood. Immediately, they started giving me a transfusion. I got several pints of blood, but I had no idea what caused it.

When I finally got out of the hospital, I went to another doctor, an internist. I told him that I'd seen a doctor a few months before and showed him all the pills that he had given me.

The internist took those pills and threw them in the trash. "We do not know what caused this," he said, "but we are going to treat it as an ulcer."

Bear in mind, this was January 1964. Doctors back then could only diagnose treatment based on what they knew at the time. So he made recommendations to my diet as if I'd had an ulcer. For a year, I could not drink coffee. Could not drink Coke. Could not drink any alcohol. All of those things would make me feel bad.

Now, let's fast-forward to the year 2015. At the recommendation of a friend, I saw a naturopath doctor in North Carolina. He asked a question that made me realize that what had happened to me fifty years earlier was a lot more than an ulcer: *Have you ever been abused?*

"Yes," I said. "For many years, when I was a little girl."

"For 90 percent of the people that see me, that answer is also yes," he said. "For most of your life, your entire nervous system has been compromised because you've been in self-defense mode."

Immediately I thought back to that night in 1964. Up to that point, I had spent almost my entire life in the grip of fear and anxiety. It was only a matter of time before everything came to a head.

* * *

Around this time, my mother flew out to Texas—not to check up on me, but to tell me that she had decided to take my sisters back with her to California. As if I didn't have enough drama in my life.

Since Vegas and California were legally and biologically the daughters of my stepfather, I knew I could not stop my mother from taking them. But I asked her to leave Jersey with me. "I'm married now," I said. "She can live with Phil and me. I don't want her going with you."

My mother said no. "He is cured now," she insisted. "He went to counseling. He's fine. Your sister is coming with me."

I did my best to change her mind, but I had no recourse. I was eighteen years old and knew absolutely nothing about life. It was hard enough just to survive and take care of myself. I was not yet equipped to take care of another person.

Still, Jersey, Vegas, and California were all upset. They didn't want to go back and live with my mother and stepfather because they knew it would be the same thing. A predator's behavior does not change.

Making matters worse, my stepfather was transferred to Japan. Since we didn't have cell phones back then, let alone personal computers and email, that made it very difficult to communicate with my siblings.

They were stationed in Japan for about two years. I wrote my mother constantly, begging her to let Jersey live with me. To no surprise, she ignored me every time.

I did get a letter from Jersey once. She told me that nothing had changed. If anything, my stepfather was even worse than he was before.

Finally, though, I got a letter from my mother telling me that they were sending Jersey to me. (My two half-sisters stayed with them.) She gave no explanation, but I didn't care. Just knowing that she'd be back with me made me happy.

My jubilation, however, was short-lived. Not long after that, my mother sent me another letter saying that Jersey was marrying a Marine.

So much for that idea, I thought.

Then it dawned on me: Jersey was older now. She was reaching the age where she was stronger and more independent and looking for a way out.

As I told you before, my stepfather always preferred much younger children.

CHAPTER NINE
Beginning Life as an Adult

There's that life. Then there's the rest of my life.

My marriage to Phil was tumultuous because of his alcoholism. Being naïve about life I did not realize the extent of his problem at the beginning of our relationship, but I quickly found out. Beyond that, I won't elaborate on our marriage because it's not pertinent to the topic of this book, except to say that he was never physically abusive to me. Thank goodness for that.

By 1967 we were married four years without any children. Like many young people, I mistakenly believed that if you had a baby, whatever problems you had with your marriage would magically be solved. That's certainly not the case.

By some miracle, however, I did get pregnant and gave birth to my daughter, Denise. From the day she was born, I knew that I would be the sole caregiver of the family. She was about eighteen months old when I decided that I could no longer deal with his drinking.

It was hard enough raising one child. I did not want to take care of two.

I told Phil that I wanted a divorce. He responded by colluding with his mother to hide Denise from me.

Once again, I didn't know what to do. I had no idea where she was, nor any resources to hire a lawyer.

One day I was sitting by the pool in our apartment complex when a woman sat beside me. Sensing my despondency, she asked how I was doing.

"Not good," I said. I explained my situation.

"I can't tell you what to do," she said, "but I can tell you what I did: You may have to pretend to get back together."

"What do you mean?" I asked.

She went on to say that, like me, she had a job. She put aside money and planned everything she needed to do, including seeing a marriage counselor, until she finally left.

"You may have to do the same thing," she said. "You may have to do all the things the marriage counselor wants you to do until you're in a position to leave."

Now I understood. For the sake of my daughter, I told Phil that I wanted us to see a marriage counselor. For the first time in my adult life, I had a plan.

The marriage counselor that Phil and I saw must have been eighty years old. She wanted to know what the problem was. I said, "I don't love him."

"First of all," she said, "I don't believe in love."

I knew then that I was in trouble.

Still, I went along and agreed with everything she suggested, and Phil and I got back together. We moved to a duplex next door to a couple who were our friends. I got a better job. I started saving money. I spent $100 on a car, a pink and gray 1955 Chevrolet that had a hole in the floorboard in the back—but it ran! I figured out a budget that covered rent, childcare, gas, food, and not much beyond that. There wasn't extra money for clothes, or even being sick. Just the bare essentials.

Then, one day in 1972, I approached Phil again and said, "I am going to tell you this one time. I am not going to stay married to you. I am going to leave. Either you and your mother can choose to fight me and think you're going to take my daughter, or you can cooperate.

"I am not here to prevent you or your family from seeing her. I want Denise to know you and your family—but I am not going to live like this anymore.

"So the choice is yours. You'll get the visitation that the court gives you, not what I will give you. I will give you more."

Fortunately, he decided not to fight me this time. After eight years of marriage, I moved out with Denise into a one-bedroom apartment upstairs. She had the bedroom. I had the couch in the living room. That was fine with me. I filed for divorce and got it.

* * *

It was in that apartment complex in Spring Branch—I want to say it was Winkler Drive Apartments—that I first met Joycelene and her son, Richard. They lived right across from me. At the time

I was working in the office for Palais Royal at Post Oak. I was looking for a better job that paid more.

Joyce was the advertising manager at ARC, an accounting records organization. She told me about a position in their accounting department. I applied for the job and they hired me.

Joycelene and I became friends. She had Richard, and I had Denise. Whenever Denise visited her dad, and Richard went to visit his dad, Joyce and I had a whole weekend to run around together, shopping and visiting friends.

That was the beginning of my life, so to speak. From that point, I started to learn how to live and enjoy life.

* * *

I met another guy. Turns out, he also had a drinking problem. I don't know why I was drawn to guys like that, but that relationship did not last long.

Around that time I met another friend who became important in my life: Mary Jo. Immediately, she and I connected. To this day, she is my spiritual friend.

I have three friends that are very special to me. My oldest friend, Myra from Hawaii, was my refuge when I was a child. I was always welcome in her family's home when I needed to get away from mine. Joycelene, whom I've just mentioned, has remained my friend since that day we met in 1972. Oh, she met Bob—and before you knew it, she was married to Bob—but she couldn't get rid of me. We've remained friends ever since.

One day, not too long ago, Joycelene and I were

talking on the phone when out of the blue she said, "You know, Barbara Jean, I never knew how to be a friend to any of my friends until I met you. I have so many friends that I took for granted, I didn't keep up with them. Eventually, I lost track of them.

"But you… you taught me what it means to really be a friend. You were always there, checking to see how things were going, giving me a shoulder to cry on. If I was sick, you were there to help me. I am so grateful for that."

I had no idea she felt that way. I didn't know what to say, except thank you.

Now that I think of it, though, I must have gotten that from my father. He was an ebullient man, outgoing and generous. He was always thinking of others. I have tried to do the same.

And then there's Mary Jo.

Mary Jo and I were both single and had children. We became each other's counselors. We would talk for hours, analyzing things. When we celebrated each other's birthdays, we would go to Courtland's and have a Velvet Hammer for our dessert. Because we didn't have a lot of money, we would take her two boys and my daughter out to Pancho's Mexican Restaurant, where they had these little flags on the tables. When you needed something, you just raised the flag and they'd bring it. It was cheap, cheap, cheap, but the kids loved going there, So that's what we did.

Eventually, I moved from Winkler Drive Apartments to the complex where Mary Jo lived. Denise started school in the Spring Branch area, further out from my first apartment. Time went on and our lives began to evolve. Relationships came and went, but all I wanted was a life with my daughter and being successful in my work. And I was. In each company I worked for, I moved up position by position by position.

One day, when Denise was about six, I felt it was important to reconnect with my family—or I should say, I felt that way about Jersey. I wanted to see her and know about her life. After a few phone conversations, we planned a get-together on the Fourth of July. Denise and I flew out to the little town where Jersey lived with her husband and their three girls, and we spent the day together. I remember her husband drove the fire truck in the parade that day. I also remember how young Jersey's daughters were. Her oldest daughter was almost the same age as Denise—they were born about a month apart. I wanted our kids to know each other. We had a nice time and everyone seemed happy.

Looking back, once again I see my father's spirit at work. I was the one who reached out and tried to make the connection happen. From what people have told me about him, I believe he would have done the same.

Granted, it's not as if Jersey and I went off in a corner and talked about our past. I didn't want to jump in there after all these years and bring up anything that would upset her. Rather, I waited for an opening from her.

As it happened, we did not discuss the past. What mattered is that we reconnected.

* * *

During the nine years when I was single again, I learned how to live in the world and become an adult for the first time. I learned what was important, what wasn't important, and how to establish values and morals. I wanted Denise to have as normal an upbringing as possible. She went to school. I went to work. When we came home, she'd do homework and we'd have dinner at a certain time. I wanted her to have a stable upbringing. That was my priority.

Yes, I had boyfriends—but in the back of my mind, I thought I'd never remarry until Denise was grown, if then. My boyfriends all knew my rules, how I operated.

In my business life, I progressed and worked as executive assistant to the vice president of international sales and marketing of a major company in Houston. I had a great job and made good money. I bought a house and, on the recommendation of my mechanics, Ron and Frank Horton, I had a new car: a Toyota Corolla, something that would last forever. I certainly didn't want a car that I would have to take in for repairs all the time. As much as I loved Ron and Frank for fixing my old red Mustang convertible over the years, I was glad to have something dependable.

Around 1978, just before Denise started sixth grade, we decided to move out of Houston. Had we stayed, she would've had to attend a school with older kids, and I did not like that environment. By that point, I was earning enough that I could afford the down payment on a brand new home in the suburb of Hockley. Denise and I moved out there, and she went to school in Waller. We were in the country, a different lifestyle.

It was a time of change in other ways, too. I

learned that Mary Jo was moving to Atlanta and take a position there. But we knew we would stay in touch.

I had not seen my mother in fourteen years, though I occasionally wrote to her. I wanted to keep up with what was happening with my siblings. By this time, Jersey and her family were now living in New Jersey. Though Dallas had stayed in touch with my mother for a while, by 1978 she had lost track of him. The last address she had for him was Lewisville, Texas. I had tried searching for him, but could not find where he was.

I never spoke to my mother on the phone, however, until I heard that she had divorced my stepfather. Now that he was out of the picture, I thought there was a possibility of healing the breach between us. I also wanted her to meet her granddaughter.

So Denise and I made a trip to California. We went to Disneyland and visited my mother and my half-sisters and their spouses for the first time.

Being a narcissist, however, my mother unloaded about all the terrible things that my stepfather had done to her. Not once did she acknowledge any of the things he had done to us—her children. Never.

From that point on, I had a limited relationship with my mother. If she needed something, then I would help her, because that's simply the right thing to do. But I never imagined that she would be in my life in a significant way again.

CHAPTER TEN
Enduring Love

In January 1979—on my birthday, in fact—I met Harold through Bob and Joyce. He and Bob had worked together and were friends for a long time. He had also separated from his wife the year before and was getting a divorce.

Bob and Joyce, in the meantime, had been looking for the right person for me for what seemed like forever. When they found out Harold was available, they decided he was the guy.

My birthday fell on a Saturday that year. I was helping Bob and Joyce in their office that day when suddenly it was time for lunch. We went across the street to this little Mexican restaurant.

Bob looked up and said, "Well, I'll be darned. Look who's here!" Harold had just walked in. They invited him to sit with us.

I, of course, had no idea that this was completely planned.

We were sitting around talking when Bob and

Joyce mentioned that we were going out that night for my birthday.

"Oh, it's your birthday?" Harold said sheepishly. (As it happened, Harold also lived in the same apartment complex as Bob and Joyce.) "If you're going out for dinner, why don't you come over to my place and have a drink before?"

They said, "OK."

Later that evening, I arrived at Bob and Joyce's place, then we went over to Harold's for drinks. He had a gift for me and he ended up joining us for dinner.

It was a nice evening. I certainly enjoyed meeting Harold—but I wasn't sure I wanted to date him because there was an age difference. But, eventually, we got past that.

Besides, life is too short to worry about things over which we have no control. What matters is that we make the most of our time and live our lives to their fullest.

Still, I didn't really start to date Harold until March. I was involved with Big Brothers and Sisters at the time, and he helped me volunteer in the booth. Later that month, he called to ask me out. I told him I couldn't. "It's my daughter's birthday," I said. "I'm taking her out skating along with her little girlfriends, and then we're going out for pizza."

Harold paused for a moment, then said, "I'd like to go with you."

Hmmm, I thought. *Maybe this guy is different.*

During the nine years when I was single, and Denise was still very young, occasionally I'd meet guys who, for the life of them, could not understand why I would be more interested in doing something with my child than in going out with them.

I remember one guy in particular. He had a lot of money, but he was also very full of himself. He called one day and said he wanted me to take me to this extravagant party on Super Bowl Sunday. To his utter surprise, I told him no. When he asked why, I explained that Super Bowl Sunday also happened to be a day on which Denise played soccer. Because I worked fulltime, there weren't many activities I could get her into. This was one of the few. Besides, on that particular Sunday, the parents were going to play the kids. It was a big deal!

Needless to say, this man was incredulous. "Are you telling me that you'd rather play soccer with your daughter than go with me to this party?"

"Yes," I said. "That's exactly what I am telling you."

I never heard from him again.

Remember, what mattered most to me was having a life with my daughter. So when Harold went skating and ate pizza that day with all these little girls, I thought to myself, *Maybe I need to give this guy a chance.*

We started dating after that. We were married on December 27, 1979.

* * *

As I look back on my life, I believe I was given strength—more strength than any of my siblings. For so many years, I had only one person to rely on: God. He was my mentor. Period.

Some people might ask, "Why did God let this happen?"

My reply is always the same: God didn't let it happen. Man let it happen. Man created this problem and allowed it to go on.

God, on the other hand, helps you, even when you don't realize it. He puts people in your life for a reason. That's why He put Harold in my life, and so many others.

CHAPTER ELEVEN
Finding My Brother

In the meantime, life went on for all of us.

Initially, my brother, Dallas, stayed in touch with my mother, at least for a while. He was married and had a daughter who was also about the same age as Denise. (He and his wife were very, very young when they met.) Then, at some point, he moved away from Lewisville, Texas and my mother lost contact with him.

Jersey, her husband, and her children flew out to visit me about a year or so after Harold and I were married. A few years after that, Denise graduated high school and went to art school. Then she got married after finishing art school. Jersey and my niece came out for the wedding, as did my mother. Eventually, Denise gave birth to my granddaughter, Brooke.

My mother and I talked occasionally on the phone. At some point, she became seriously ill and required surgery. She asked me to fly out to California and take care of her when she went in for surgery. Even though I had two half-sisters out there who could have done that for her, I flew out and spent ten days with her until she was OK.

After that time, we had a small reunion at my sister's home in New Jersey. Harold and I flew out from Texas, while both my half-sisters came out from California. No one talked about anything that had happened to us as children.

Meanwhile, Jersey and her husband had some property next to their house in New Jersey. They offered it to my mother. Knowing how expensive it was to live in California, my mother wanted to take them up on their offer. She called and asked me what I thought.

I told her that if they were giving her the land to build a house on, it would save her money in the long run, because she wouldn't have to worry about mortgage payments. "So it's probably a good idea," I said.

Next thing you know, my mother sold her house and relocated to New Jersey. My grandparents in California were furious. For years, I did not understand why. Then I learned the back story.

After my mother divorced my stepfather, she wanted to get all her teeth taken care of—a procedure that cost a lot of money. My grandmother made her a deal: She would pay for my mother's teeth, provided that my mother agreed to live in Hayward (or, at least, somewhere in the vicinity of Hayward) for as long as my maternal grandparents were alive. That way, as my grandparents aged, they would have someone from their `ohana on whom they could depend. (In Hawaii, the family is your `ohana. It is a tradition that families remain bound together and remember one another.)

Being a narcissist, my mother didn't tell my grandparents that she was moving to New Jersey until after her house was sold. Oh, my goodness, was there a scene.

Granted, my grandmother in her younger years was not a great person. Anytime I've mentioned her name to anyone that knew her, the response is always the same: "Oh, that hateful old woman. She was the worst." She was extremely controlling. Knowing what I've come to know about my mother's upbringing, I'm sure she suffered at her hand—in fact, I know she did. For instance, when my mother was young, my grandmother would often lock my mother under the house (along with one of my mother's sisters) and then go out somewhere. She really put the fear of God in them.

My maternal grandmother was also a real drama queen. One time, she and my maternal grandfather had a real doozy of an argument. My grandmother yelled and screamed at him before collapsing on the floor, as if she had fainted.

By this point in their marriage, my maternal grandfather knew fully well that his wife was prone to such bizarre histrionics as pretending to faint just to get her way. He was therefore pretty certain that this was just another act. However, my mother, still being a young girl at the time, was genuinely concerned. Pointing to the sight of my grandmother sprawled out on the floor, she pleaded to my maternal grandfather to do something.

Without skipping a beat, my maternal grandfather went over to the sink, poured himself a glass of water and threw it on my grandmother's face.

Immediately she jumped off the floor and began coughing and sputtering while staring at him indignantly. Sure enough, it was all an act, and my maternal grandfather knew it. (My maternal grandfather died in the 1940s. My maternal grandmother remarried.)

My mother also told me that, while she was pregnant with me, my grandmother once hit her with such force, she fell down the back steps. That's the kind of thing that my grandmother did in her day. Growing up as a child, I knew my grandmother could get mad, and I knew she could be extremely controlling over my mother—but I never saw *that* side of her.

Still, family patterns often repeat themselves. When you consider that she herself was raised by a narcissist, it's not surprising that my mother went back on her promise to my grandmother and thought only of herself.

* * *

While my mother lived in New Jersey, Harold and I moved into our house in Cypress, a suburb of Houston. By this time, I had spent the previous year trying to find my brother. We'd watch different shows on TV about family members searching for each other. That always made me think of my brother.

Some friends of ours had a daughter who had just moved to the Dallas area. One Sunday, I asked for their daughter's phone number. She wasn't there when I called, but I spoke to her fiancé. I asked him to look in the Dallas phone book to see if anyone listed here had my family's last name.

"There's only one," he said.

I asked for the number. When I called, I told the person who answered who I was and that I was looking for my brother. I gave his full name.

There was a long silence on the other end of the line. Finally, the woman said, "That's my father. I have my sisters here and we have been talking about going on Oprah Winfrey to find you."

Thank God that didn't happen, I thought. *I would have died.*

I left her my number. When my brother called me back that day, I decided to see him in Dallas, which I did a few days later. By that time he had remarried, though that marriage did not last long. (I won't go into details, except to say that his second wife was not a good influence on him.)

I called my mother and told her that I had found him. She was very excited. Once we knew where he was, she, Jersey, and my half-sisters all flew out to see him. Harold and I rented a van and drove everyone from Houston. During that same trip, as long as my family was still in town, we also arranged for a reunion at our home in Cypress. Dallas drove out for that.

I cannot tell you how good it felt to see my brother again. After all these years, he was the missing link in reconnecting our family.

What I did not know at the time was that, thanks to my mother, my brother had come to believe that I had never wanted to find him—and that the only reason I looked for him was because she wanted me to. When I finally learned that many years later, I was shocked, and yet not completely surprised.

CHAPTER TWELVE
Mom's Relocation

When my mother moved to New Jersey, she lived with my sister and her husband for about a year while her house was being built. Though it took a while to adjust to the weather back east (and particularly the snow and cold), she was happy with her new house and her yard once everything was finished. Life was good initially, until little cracks appeared on the surface.

Once my mother moved into her own place, Jersey thought everything would be fine. But then she started calling me, complaining that our mother was "constantly" in their lives and that they "couldn't breathe." Every day, as soon as Jersey and her husband got home from work, my mother would call them for one reason or another. Sometimes she would arrive unannounced. Before long Jersey and her entire family started sneaking in at night, hoping to avoid her. It even got to the point where they would keep the lights off at night, so as not to alert her that they were home.

Meanwhile, by this time I had quit my job with a well-known oil services company and helped Harold run his engineering business. This was in 1989. When Harold first started his company, he worked in an office that provided secretarial service. As time went on, and his business continued to grow, it was clear he would need his own employees, so I encouraged him to hire a receptionist. Then he added another person. Then it became very apparent that he needed me to help him, so I did.

Before I got there, Harold had no office systems or procedures in place. He kept pretty much everything in an A-Z folder (or in his head). When I came on board, since I had a strong background in administrative, finance and accounting, I took over that part of the operation. I implemented procedures for sales, purchasing, and production, created forms and guidelines, handled all legal and insurance, and ran the office on a day-to-day basis. That way, Harold could focus on engineering sales and production.

It was also around this time that Harold's mother, Lela, came to live with us. She was eighty-nine years old and no longer wanted to live alone. She had been living in Dallas. Though she had many friends, which was a good thing, as she continued to age, she needed more help with day-to-day living.

By then, we were living in Cypress. Our house there had a guest house—a full apartment, really—next to the garage. I told Lela that the place was hers if she wanted it. She gladly accepted. I think when she moved there she thought that, since she would be near her grandchildren, they would come to see her all the time. Well, that didn't turn out quite the way she imagined it would: After all, her grandchildren had lives of their own. But she kept herself busy with her plants and her books and other activities. She was a Christian Scientist and went to church on Sunday. She was often on the phone, talking to her friends in Dallas. She stayed with us for seven years, then spent another two years in assisted living. During that time, I spent as much time with her as I could.

Sometimes we'd go to a movie. I particularly remember taking her to see *Mrs. Doubtfire* with Robin Williams. There were not a lot of movies that Lela approved of, but she absolutely loved that one. She laughed through the whole thing.

One time, around 1995, Joyce and I took Lela on a trip to Galveston, along with Joyce's mother and stepfather. That was another experience! Lela was very tall and a big woman. If she fell down, you were hard-pressed to get her back up. Even Harold had difficulty lifting her.

We once went to Moody Gardens to see the butterfly exhibit. When Joyce pulled up in her van, her mother, Geri, jumped out, as did her stepfather, Pete. Lela was on the far side. By this time, she was in her nineties. When she went to get into the other seat beside the door, she fell down between the seats.

Oh, no, I thought. *How are we going to get her up?*

I went behind Lela and hooked my arm around under hers and got her on that other seat. To this day, I still don't know how I did it! Fortunately, though, we all had a really good laugh about it.

After seeing the butterfly exhibit, we had an extra treat. The TV miniseries *A Woman of Independent Means*, starring Sally Fields, was being filmed on location that day at the Strand in Galveston. Though we did not have a chance to say hello to Sally Fields, we were allowed to observe her acting for a while. I remember thinking how thin she was!

Then everyone decided that they wanted to ride the trolley next. We got them in the trolley, no problem—but when it was time to exit, Lela couldn't step down. She had to sit and come down the steps like a child would on her butt.

I mentioned that Lela spent the last two years of her life in assisted living. There was a practical reason for that: Because Harold and I had our own business, we were often on the road. Too many times, something would happen and we'd have to come back. One time she had fallen and the friends who were looking in on her had a hard time lifting her up.

* * *

Sometime after Lela went into assisted living, I spoke with my mother. Once again she was complaining about her life in New Jersey.

Of course, with my mother, you really had to read between the lines because not everything she said was true. I knew that because, unbeknownst to my mother, I was also communicating with Jersey at the time, so I heard both sides of the story.

In any event, one time I was on the phone, telling my mother that I was planning a trip to Hawaii. I hadn't seen or heard from any of my family since 1959, and I wanted to reconnect with them. I invited her to go with me.

"Why would you want me to go?" she asked.

I told her that she knew her way around (at least, I thought she did), and I didn't. She thought about it and said yes.

We stayed in a hotel. I saw my aunt and my cousins. None of them knew what had happened to us from the time we left—they got bits and pieces of stories from my grandmother, but for the most part, they had no clue.

I reconnected with my cousin, Laverne. She was a few years younger than me, but when we were kids, whenever our families got together, she and I were inseparable. Well, wouldn't you know, even though we hadn't seen each other in years Laverne and I picked up right where we had left off.

At one point we had an opportunity to sit and talk, just the two of us. "Whatever happened to all of you when you left Hawaii?" she asked. So I told her.

"Now everything makes sense," she said. "We knew something wasn't right, but we didn't know what it was. Why didn't you contact us?"

"I had no means by which to do that," I said.

That was the truth. My mother and stepfather had isolated us from the rest of my father's family. I had no phone numbers, no addresses, nothing.

"I know my father would have immediately gone and got all of you," Laverne said. "He would have brought you here and we would have taken care of you."

During this trip, Laverne also put me back in touch with my half-sister, Ethel, and my half-brother, Donald. They were my father's children from his first marriage. I hadn't seen or spoken to them since I was three and a half years old. I immediately contacted them both once I returned to Texas. The three of us arranged for a reunion in California, where Donald lived.

For a short time when he was a kid, Donald lived with our dad and my mother in the garage apartment. (I have a picture with him when I was two or three.) I told him what had happened to us, but I'm not sure it registered. I'm sure he believed that there had to be a reason why my mother couldn't come forward.

Ethel, on the other hand, never cared for my mother. She was about eighteen or nineteen when my mother married my father. (I believe Donald was fourteen or fifteen at the time.) So when I told her what happened to us, it made her even angrier that my mother allowed this to happen.

Ethel may be only a half-sister, but I am closer to her than I am with any of my other siblings. God has always been important in her life, just as He has been for my father and me. But she also knows that He does not want us to continue hating someone for the rest of our lives. It took a long time for her to do it, but, eventually, she was able to let go of the anger and hate that she had for my mother.

* * *

Meanwhile, Jersey was not happy in her marriage. Sad to say, I was not surprised. She got married in Japan when she was very young and still living with my mother and stepfather. She married her husband simply because she saw it as her opportunity to finally escape that house.

Granted, I did not choose wisely with my first marriage, either. But, at least, I learned from my mistakes and was able to figure life out first before I tried again.

Jersey, unfortunately, never had that opportunity.

Instead, she just went from living at home, with no experience with dating or asking herself if she really loved this person, to suddenly being married. Oh, she loved her husband and cared for him, but she wasn't in love with him. Then she immediately had children and wasn't ready for that, either. Eventually, after many years, she ended up getting a divorce.

Unfortunately, Jersey was not strong enough or knowledgeable enough to live on her own. She met a guy at work and, before too long, ended up marrying him. Her children weren't excited about this, but they accepted it.

Once they were married, Jersey sold her house, and she and her husband moved to Atlantic City. My mother did not like that development at all.

Bear in mind, all of this had transpired after my mother and I went to Hawaii. On the plane ride back from Hawaii, my mother told me that she wanted to move back to Hawaii. Though my mother said that she "really wanted" to live in the same apartment building where my aunt lived, the real impetus, apparently, was her belief that Jersey was eventually moving to Atlantic City and away from her.

My mother, being a narcissist, suddenly felt abandoned.

Still, her decision to move to Hawaii surprised me. Given her upbringing, my mother always wanted the best of everything—her home, her things, everything. While my aunt's apartment is a nice place, it was certainly not like any of the homes in which my mother had lived before. But it was the only place my aunt could afford after my uncle died.

I suppose, deep down, my mother wanted to move back to her home in Hawaii and away from all her memories. A new life with no children, so to speak.

My mother even had the paperwork with her and showed it to me on the plane. Apparently, my aunt had helped her. So when we got home, I called Jersey and told her that Mom was moving to Hawaii.

"No, she isn't," said Jersey.

"Yes, she is," I said.

"Oh, no, she isn't," said Jersey. "She's not going to do that." She could not believe that my mother would leave the extremely nice spacious house she had built.

I never really understood that. For more than seven years my sister did nothing but complain about our mother living so close by. But, for whatever reason, she didn't want her to move to Hawaii.

Then again, happy or not, Jersey could not cut the bond with my mother. Neither could any of my other siblings. It wasn't just the strength of the mother/daughter connection. I just don't think they ever completely grasped what she had done to us— that she could have stopped our stepfather from abusing us, but instead looked the other way.

Of course, being a narcissist my mother thought only of herself. Before too long she relocated back to Hawaii.

Once again, things were good initially. In Hawaii, the family is so tightly knit, you know every inch of each other's lives, and what's going on with their family members. So when my mother moved back there, my aunt and my cousins helped her with whatever she needed, because she was family. (My mother, of course, loved that, because it made her the center of attention.)

My mother lived upstairs from my aunt; eventually, she moved downstairs. She had an apartment with a patio and a front yard, so she was able to have her plants. (Gardening was always her thing.) Occasionally, some of us would fly out to Hawaii to visit her over the years.

My mother wasted no time telling the family stories about each of her children. She gave them the impression that she did not really love her children, and she did not hesitate to imply that her children took advantage of her.

CHAPTER THIRTEEN
Manipulation

In January 1999, my maternal grandmother became ill with pneumonia. Before long, however, it became apparent that she would not recover. We put her in a nursing home in February, and she passed away a few weeks later. Throughout this time, I traveled back and forth to California to help out while I was still working with Harold.

After my grandmother died, I helped my stepgrandfather with the funeral arrangements. By that point, though, they had already picked everything out.

Sometime later, my stepgrandfather said that he wanted to move to Texas. He wanted to have his own place, but he also wanted to be close to me in case he ever needed help. So he flew out to Houston and we found a place called The Terrace, a senior resident community where he could pretty much live independently. He would have an apartment and his own car. The Terrace offered a small breakfast every day, while the main meal was lunch. The residents were then free to make their own dinner. They also had various activities and the people who lived there really got to know each other. All in all, it was a good environment, so he decided to live there.

My stepgrandfather went back to California, put his home on the market, and sold everything else. Meanwhile, I went ahead and bought new furniture for his new apartment so that it would be ready by the time he moved in. Then, in December, I went back to California, loaded my stepgrandfather's car, and we drove back to Texas. He lived at The Terrace for five years and was very happy there before he passed in 2005.

In the meantime, Harold and I continued to work many long hours to make our company successful. By the end of 2001, however, the stress was beginning to get to him. He had a mini-stroke. I knew we needed to sell the company. It took several months of prolonged negotiations—and, knowing Harold's condition, I spent many hours praying about it and had my church pray about it, too—but, eventually, we made a deal in September 2002. Harold stayed with the company under the new ownership for about another two years before retiring in 2005. During that time, I worked with the builders on our house on the lake. We moved into that house in 2005 and lived there until 2017.

* * *

Before she moved to Hawaii, my mother wanted to do a simple will. Because she had already sold her house and did not have any other property to speak of, I got one of those forms from Office Depot. She wanted to invest some of her money, so I took her down to Washington Mutual and we put it in an investment in Texas. The rest of her money, she took with her to Hawaii. We did the will and had it notarized. She lived in Hawaii for about ten years.

During that period, I started to realize that my mother was basically two people: The one I knew and the one who could charm the pants off people who didn't know any better. Meaning, my mother was nothing if not manipulative—a trait she had learned from my maternal grandmother. (My maternal stepgrandfather, on the other hand, was far more good-natured and, therefore, a little more gullible. He knew how to handle money all right, but he was never good at reading people. In fact, at one point, after my grandmother died, he was nearly swindled by someone who took advantage of his good nature. Fortunately, after a call from my cousin, I intervened and steered him out of trouble. Not long after that, my stepgrandfather moved to Texas.)

My mother was the type of person who liked to stir things up, particularly among her own children. I say this not to denigrate her, but simply to give you some insight into how she was wired. She had no qualms about pitting one child against the other. Whichever child she talked to, she wanted them to adore her and believe every word she said. So, after telling So and So whatever he or she wanted to hear, she would move on to the next child and tell them that she completely disapproved of So and So's lifestyle. Or, if So and So had confided in her about one of us, she would immediately betray their confidence.

Because my mother was a narcissist, I suppose that it never dawned on her that my siblings and I might actually talk to each other and realize what she was doing. For example, when she lived on the East Coast near my sister, Jersey, my mother would tell me all these stories about Jersey and her children that simply were not true—I knew that, because I had kept in touch with Jersey and knew what the problems were. I could see right through my mother because I always listened to everything.

Sadly, like the rest of my siblings, Jersey had a blind spot for my mother. Despite everything that had happened to us, they all idolized her. That has never ceased to amaze me. But I understand why.

When my mother lived in Hawaii, she did the same thing to my cousins and relatives over there, pitting one against the other. At one point, things got so toxic that it affected my aunt's health.

The turning point in their relationship had to do with a car. My mother and my aunt each owned a car, but my aunt's was not very reliable. For some inexplicable reason, my mother decided to give my aunt her car. But, because no good deed goes unpunished, my aunt essentially had to chauffeur my mother for all her errands and appointments.

My aunt did not mind doing that initially because they had more or less worked out a schedule. Then my mother started arbitrarily changing the schedule without telling my aunt. She expected my aunt to do her bidding, literally at a moment's notice. That was a big part of the conflict. Then it came down to insurance.

At first, even though she had given the car to my

aunt, my mother insisted on paying for everything, including insurance. Then, all of a sudden, she changed her mind about handling the insurance payments—without telling my aunt.

My aunt was living only on Social Security. She did not have a lot of money. One day she received a notice from the insurance company saying that the policy on the car was three months in arrears. You can imagine how alarmed she was when she suddenly realized that my mother expected her to pay it.

Naturally, my mother called me to complain about how irresponsible my aunt was. What she didn't know, of course, is that I knew both sides of the story because I had kept in contact with my aunt.

Long story short, I went to Hawaii, sat them both down along with one of my cousins, and we worked out an arrangement. From then on, my aunt was no longer responsible for my mother. If my mother needed anything from K-Mart or the nearby grocery store, she would walk. Otherwise, my cousin would drive her.

* * *

Then my mother started using her health as a weapon. She particularly began to complain all the time that her heart was getting bad. (Kind of like what Fred Sanford did every week on *Sanford and Son*. Whenever Lamont caught on to his latest shenanigans, Fred would clutch his chest and pretend he was "having the Big One." It was always a diversionary tactic.)

Granted, my mother did have a pacemaker put in some years before, so her heart was not in the greatest condition. But it got to the point where we were always trying to figure out what was real and what wasn't. This was particularly tricky once my mother started having other medical problems. In particular, she kept falling and hurting herself.

Compounding the matter was that my cousin's husband, Armon, happened to manage the building where my mother lived. Armon informed the tenants that they could no longer live in their apartment on their own if they were falling. They would either need a roommate or have to move somewhere else.

One day my mother came home from K-Mart all covered in blood. Not wanting to lose her apartment (or her independence), she said that someone had thrown a rock and hit her. Armon walked down to the spot where this incident supposedly took place and determined that it could not have happened according to my mother's story. The only explanation, he and I deduced, was that she had fallen again.

There were other incidents when my aunt or my cousin or someone else would discover my mother had fallen. Rather than admit what had happened, however, my mother would concoct another story. Finally, after one such episode, Armon called to tell me that something had to be done: She needed to move to an assisted living home or have someone live with her.

I phoned my mother and told her that she had to make a decision. I suggested that I fly out to Hawaii and help her find a place with other seniors. "Either that, or you could move into a two-bedroom apartment there and get Jersey or Vegas to look after you."

My mother immediately shot down the second

idea. "Jersey can't come because of her job," she explained. "She has already told me that. She doesn't want to lose her retirement benefits and her house isn't big enough for me to go and live with her.

As for Vegas or California, my half-sisters, my mother had already dismissed them as an option. That story stems from the time when Vegas had decided to visit her in Hawaii.

As it happens, Harold and I had also flown out for a visit, so we witnessed everything. Even though Vegas was her daughter (by my stepfather), my mother treated her terribly and made no bones about it. Eventually, Vegas confided in me: "It's as if my mother doesn't even love me."

I finally confronted my mother and said, "You need to stop. If you don't want Vegas here, you need to send her back."

For the remainder of her trip, Vegas stayed with my cousin, without any understanding of why my mother treated her that way. But that was truly how my mother felt about Vegas and California.

I suspect my mother grew to resent my half-sisters because they were my stepfather's children. This was particularly true after the divorce. She absolutely hated him because of the position he left her in and how he left her.

Not once did it occur to my mother to be angry at my stepfather or have any outrage over any of the things that he had done to us—*her own children*. Being a narcissist, she was incapable of having empathy for anyone but herself. Rather than accept responsibility for the victims she helped create, she turned her back on her own daughters and pretended that they were a problem.

My half-sisters had a lot of problems as a result of their father. Instead of recognizing that, my mother blamed them for their poor choices in life.

* * *

My mother knew that she had to move, but she made no decision that night. Instead, when we got off the phone, she said she would think about it.

Of course, there was one other option—though, truth be told, that thought never really crossed my mind because I knew it would be too weird. But, apparently, it was not too weird of an idea for my mother.

She called about a week later. "I want to move to Texas where you are," she said.

My mother knew that our house at the lake had a private apartment with a patio. She also knew that Harold's mother, Lela, had once lived with us. She thought it would be the perfect place for her.

"Are you sure you want to do this?" I asked.

"Yes," she said. "I want to do this."

Still… I had to really think about this. My mother, who had never protected me as a child, was now asking me to take care of her.

True, we did help Lela for nine years. That was a good situation, though, because Lela had a full life. Unlike my mother, Lela was a woman of faith. She was very active with her church and enjoyed reading her Bible. She had her friends in Dallas, with whom she communicated every day, plus she went to church with our neighbor next door because they were of the same faith. She was a content, happy person who liked living with us and appreciated being close to family.

My mother, on the other hand, was none of the above. If Harold and I took her in, this promised to be an entirely different situation.

CHAPTER FOURTEEN
Moving My Mother

My mother's health was another factor. I was aware of her falling episodes. But, apparently, she was also having mini-strokes. I knew that she really could not live by herself anymore.

Still, I prayed on the matter and remembered God's Word: Honor your father and mother. So, in April 2008, I decided that I would do what I could to take care of her.

Then again, this being my mother, I also knew that nothing about this would be easy. For one, she wanted to move right away. There was no way I could do that. I had to take care of a few things so that I could plan for her arrival. Plus I figured that I would have to fly out to Hawaii first and help her sell her furniture and other belongings that she would no longer need once she moved to Texas. (Remember, Harold and I had a fully furnished guesthouse.) It would be at least a month before I could do that.

Then I found out that Jersey and her daughter

were flying out to see my mother in July. I suggested that we postpone the move until after their visit.

"I don't want to see them," my mother said coldly. "I don't want to be here when they come."

We went back and forth on this before she finally agreed to call Jersey and tell her that she was leaving Hawaii. I certainly didn't want this to fall back on me.

In hindsight, I should have made that call myself instead of trusting my mother to do it. But we'll get to that later.

* * *

My mother also promised that she would not get rid of anything until I arrived at her place at the end of May. I should have known better about that, too. Sure enough, by the time I got there, my mother had already sold darn near everything. Her suitcases and all of her boxes were packed.

I asked her why she didn't wait. "I just wanted to hurry up and get this done," she said.

At that point, it only took two weeks to finalize the rest of the things that needed to be done: going to the doctor, getting her records, going to the social security office, transferring all her banking. We left toward the end of June and came to Montgomery, Texas.

Then, a few weeks later, my aunt told me that Jersey and her daughter and her daughter's family had flown to Hawaii to visit my mother—and couldn't believe that she had moved! My mother had never bothered to tell them. They had gone to all that expense to see her and she wasn't even there.

Yes, that is unconscionable. But my mother did

that kind of stuff all the time. Anything she wanted to do, she went ahead and did it, without ever taking responsibility. Being a narcissist, she would always blame someone else.

Which brings us to the story of why Jersey no longer speaks to me.

From what I understand, Jersey once told my mother that if she ever moved to Texas, she would never speak to her again. For some reason, she did not want her here, living with us.

I would not learn this until much later, but, apparently, my mother told Jersey that I had "made her" give up her apartment and come to Texas.

Never mind the fact that it was *my mother* who had asked me to take her in. She liked to pit us against each other. That's just the way she was.

Jersey convinced her children that I deliberately moved my mother so that they could not see her. That makes no sense—but, in a lot of ways, Jersey is a lot like my mother.

* * *

At first, my mother liked her new surroundings—especially the backyard. Knowing how much she loved to garden, I told her that she could work in the backyard to her heart's content.

Then she realized that she wouldn't have people living nearby to converse with and tell stories to, like she did in Hawaii. The houses in our neighborhood aren't conducive to that sort of environment because they're spread further apart.

That wasn't going to work for my mother. She needed people to be close to her so that she could manipulate them.

Because Harold and I were retired and living very well, my mother never had to pay for anything here except her spending money. If there was a neighborhood function or activity, we'd take her with us. From time to time, I'd take her to the movies. I did all the same things with her that I did with Lela: hair appointments, doctors, shopping. The only difference was the constant calls from my sister to my mother. Their conversations were usually the same: My mother would say that she didn't have a lot of people to talk to. My sister would reply, "Why did you move?"

I'm sure that Jersey took advantage of every opportunity to make my mother feel unhappy and that my mother took advantage of every opportunity to complain. As time went on, things became even more difficult.

One day my mother couldn't wait to show me the Mother's Day card she received from my half-sister California. I'm sure she wanted me to read it because of how mushy it was.

"I think about all the happy times we had together," California wrote in the card. "You were such a wonderful mother…"

Forget that the fact my mother treated California as badly as she did my half-sister Vegas. These "happy times" that California wrote about simply did not happen. Not in the house that I grew up in. Certainly not with my stepfather under the same roof.

Here I had a sister who wasn't speaking to me, and a half-sister who was living in total denial. That just blew my mind.

* * *

Throughout the time my mother lived with us, I kept in touch with my brother, Dallas. Like my other siblings, he never talked about the past; to this day, I believe his kids know nothing about the past. One day, however, he told me a story that shed light on the type of person my mother was.

Dallas' daughter, from his first wife, was born in November 1967. (As it happens, that was also around the time when Jersey had her daughter and I had Denise.) Not long after his child's birth, Dallas decided to visit my mother so that she could see her first granddaughter. When he called, however, my mother had a strange response: "I don't want you to come here."

Now, keep in mind that my mother was still married to my stepfather in 1968. By that point, however, all of her children had grown up and left the house. It was just the two of them living together.

Not long after telling my brother not to visit her, my mother called him back and dropped another bombshell. "We want to take your daughter," she said. "You can't afford to take care of her and raise her."

When Dallas told me that, my blood ran cold. I simply could not believe it.

My mother knew what kind of person my stepfather was. She knew what he had done to all of us. Yet she wanted to bring her granddaughter into their house so that he could prey upon her, just as he had sexually abused my siblings and me.

Then it dawned on me: My stepfather was the breadwinner. My mother never held a paid job during the entire time she was married to him. Like my maternal grandmother before her, she was motivated by money and material possessions. The only reason she wanted Dallas' daughter was the same reason why she looked the other way whenever my stepfather abused us: My mother wanted to protect her livelihood. Otherwise, she was afraid that my stepfather would leave her.

* * *

During the years she lived with Harold and me, my mother would occasionally say other things that made me take pause. One time, when I was alone with her, I asked her a question about her and my stepfather. In the course of her response, she said that "none of us"—meaning her, my sisters, and me— "ever spoke up to him. Everything had to be as he wanted it. You couldn't object. We just did what we were supposed to."

I said, "I spoke up to him."

She had no response for that. Instead, she kept referring to herself as a victim, as if all along she was no different than we were.

I remember how I kept shaking my head when I told Harold about this.

My mother was never afraid of my stepfather. She just never wanted to cross that line that would risk losing her financial dependence. How could she make herself a victim?

A mother is supposed to protect her children, not put them in harm's way. What on earth was she really saying?

Then again, by that point in her life, my mother

was so deep in denial, she could not dig herself out. Clearly, she had blocked the truth about her actions completely out of her mind.

I will never understand my mother's behavior, but I do feel sad for her. She lacked the moral and loving foundation to create a loving family.

CHAPTER FIFTEEN
Things Begin to Unravel

My mother moved in with us in the summer of 2008. As was her nature, she created drama wherever she went. That progressively took its toll on me physically, to the point where I started having chest pains in early 2010. When I went to my doctor for a checkup, he took my blood pressure and said it was through the roof.

Knowing that I had always had very low blood pressure, he asked, "What is going on with you?"

I knew what the problem was. The same thing happened to my aunt when she lived next to my mother in Hawaii. It was emotional stress from dealing with all of the drama caused by my mother.

It wasn't just me. Harold was also becoming depressed because we no longer had a life. We didn't do things and go out to places like we used to do. He felt his life was stifled. We needed to do something. We had to find another place for my mother to live.

Problem was, we both knew that my mother

could no longer live on her own.

I called my cousin Laverne. "Why can't one of the others help take care of your mother?" she asked. "You've done it all these years." She suggested my half-sister Vegas.

My instinct told me that was a bad idea.

Granted, of all my siblings, Vegas was the only one who admitted she was "screwed up" (as she put it) because of her father—my stepfather—and the things he had done. Even though she had a blind devotion to my mother (despite how poorly my mother treated her over the years), I wasn't sure this was going to work.

My cousin, however, convinced me otherwise. She had visited Vegas a couple of times in recent months and Vegas told her that she wanted to turn her life around. Laverne sincerely believed that Vegas deserved another chance, and so did I.

Not only that, Vegas had worked before as a CNA—a certified nursing assistant. What better person could there be to live with our mother?

I called Vegas and asked her if she would come to Texas and take care of our mother. She said yes. Then I told my mother, "I'm going to find another place for you to live. I don't think you're happy here, since you don't have anyone your age around you."

My mother didn't argue that point. Of course, Jersey had long since convinced her that she was not happy living with me.

I found a very nice adult, senior complex: a fenced-in community with a duplex that had two bedrooms, two baths, a dining room, a living room and a patio in the front. It also had security. I took my mother to the duplex and she liked it.

Then I told her that Vegas was coming to live with her. To my surprise, that was fine with her—despite the fact that, when she was living in Hawaii and needed someone to help her, my mother adamantly opposed the idea of Vegas living with her. (That would've been the simplest arrangement: My mother could have stayed in Hawaii, Vegas could have lived with her there in a two-bedroom apartment, and all of this turmoil would have been avoided. But, because my mother could never do anything in her life without creating conflict for others, that obviously did not happen.)

* * *

There was another complication with Vegas: Even though she worked in elder care (and therefore seemed to understand all of the responsibilities she would have to undertake once she started living with my mother), because of the psychological damage caused by her father—my stepfather—she was emotionally immature. I didn't realize how immature she was, however, until I moved her here.

Had I known then what I know now, I never, ever would've consented to this. I would have looked for another arrangement for my mother, even if that meant moving her back to Hawaii and finding a place for her there.

Vegas moved to Texas in the middle of February 2010. Two weeks later, in March of that year, I moved my mother into the duplex. I furnished and set up the whole place. It looked great, if I may say so myself.

This was not supposed to be a job for Vegas—

like I said, it was a responsibility. She had free rent, food, gas, and living expenses. Not only that, but once my mother passed, she could continue to live there and eventually inherit the place.

My mother was only there a couple of months when Vegas phoned me in a panic. "I don't know what's wrong with Mom. She has fallen and she is on the floor. I can't lift her because of my back."

I raced over there. My mother had had another mini-stroke. I lifted her enough to get into her chair in the living room.

Now I had a problem. Clearly, Vegas was nowhere near as qualified as I thought she was, physically or mentally.

I called my mother's doctor. "You really need to call either Visiting Angels or hospice and get them involved at this point," he said.

I opted to call hospice. I went over and discussed my mother's situation. Even with Vegas taking care of her, someone with a medical background would have to check on her.

"That is what we do," they said. "It is called Palliative Care."

* * *

In the beginning, when my mother first moved to Texas, she had two bank accounts. One was where her Social Security check was deposited, while the other was a small pension fund. I took care of the second account and used it to pay all of her bills: rent, electricity, everything.

Wishing to be fair to Vegas, Harold and I decided to put her name on the first account. That way, she would have some freedom. She smoked, so she could use the funds in that account to buy cigarettes, dog food (for her dog), in addition to groceries. I collected the receipts and canceled checks tied to that account for tax purposes.

One day, as I started looking through those receipts, I noticed that Vegas would go to the store, buy a bunch of groceries—then two days later, go back to the store and spend $250 for the exact same items. That made no sense to me. What on earth was she doing? Was she buying food for someone? Who was she benefiting?

I did not want to come out and ask because Vegas could've said anything. But things began to spiral downward from that point on.

Meanwhile, I continued to visit my mother every week. As the weeks and months went by, however, I could see a drastic change in her. She was no longer going out. She wasn't even changing her clothes anymore. Beyond going from her chair to her bed and back every day, she was completely immobile and had no interaction with others. Clearly, something was not right.

In November 2011, Vegas complained about how my mother always fell whenever she got out of bed. Hospice suggested that Harold and I get her a hospital bed, which we did.

Finally, in early December 2011, I got another call from Vegas. All she did was yell and scream, "I can't do this anymore. I can't do this anymore."

I contacted the attorney that had drawn up my mother's will shortly after she had moved to Texas. I explained that she had given me powers of attorney for her health and other matters for the past fifteen years. I told him that I had reason to believe that Vegas was doing something underhanded. I wanted to make sure that my mother's interests were protected.

"About the only thing you can do is to apply for full guardianship," he said. "But I wouldn't advise it because family members get upset."

Clearly, this man was not going to help me.

"But my mother is not in her right mind," I pleaded.

He said, "You need to have her evaluated."

I called my mother's doctor, this time to make an appointment. I wanted to have her evaluated. When I called Vegas to tell her, she became nervous and defensive. "Why is she going to the doctor?" she asked.

"Because he wants to evaluate her," I said.

A few days later, in January 2012, Harold and I came by to take my mother to the doctor. Vegas and her boyfriend were sitting on the couch. "Mom doesn't want to go," she said.

"She is going to the doctor," I said. This was not a matter for discussion.

I went into my mother's room. What Vegas said was not true: My mother seemed perfectly fine with the idea of going. I went to help her out of bed, but because she had been confined to her bed so much since November, everything hurt. When I lifted her, she winced.

"You don't know what you're doing," Vegas snapped. "You don't know how to handle her."

"Fine," I said. "You do it."

Vegas got my mother out of the bed and put her in the wheelchair. I wheeled my mother to the car.

Harold and I put her in the back seat. We were about ready to leave when Vegas suddenly said, "I'm going, too."

"Fine," I said. "Get in the back seat." She did. Her boyfriend followed in his pickup truck.

When we got to the doctor's office, Vegas sat next to my mom in the waiting room and cried.

What in the heck is she doing now? I wondered. She was acting like a teenager. Mentally, she was.

I told the nurse that when the doctor was ready to see my mother, I wanted no one else in the examining room but him and her. She said, "We can do that."

Naturally, when they came to get my mom, Vegas insisted on joining her. "No," said the nurse. "He wants to see her by himself."

They led her into the examining room. A few minutes later, the doctor came to the door and motioned me to come in. I got up and went inside. Sure enough, Vegas also tried to bully her way in there.

The doctor looked at me and said, "Do you want her in here?"

I said, "No." That was that. Vegas had to stay in the waiting room.

The doctor told me that my mother was in major dementia. On a scale of 1 to 10, with 1 being good and 10 being bad, she was a 9.

"Can you write me a letter to that effect?" I asked.

"Yes," he said, "I sure can."

That was on a Wednesday. I took my mother home and went back to get the letter on Friday, which was my birthday. At that point, I had already started looking for a place to move her. Now that I knew she had dementia, she needed better care than what Vegas could provide.

Around five o'clock that same day, Harold and I were about to leave for a family dinner when I got a phone call from the bank. Vegas had closed my mother's bank account.

What Vegas didn't realize is that I had instructed the bank in writing that if anyone tried to make changes to my mother's account, the bank was to alert me. Needless to say, I was livid.

Then I learned that Vegas had some lawyer come to the house to interview my mother.

Remember, my mother was nearly in full-blown dementia. In no way was she capable of making financial decisions. (The problem with dementia is that people can seem normal at times, and not normal at other times.) Even if she was capable of making a financial decision, the *last* thing she would do is turn her money over to Vegas because she did not trust her.

Problem was, it was five o'clock on Friday afternoon. There was nothing I could do about it until Monday.

CHAPTER SIXTEEN
A Turn For The Worse

Long story short, I hired an attorney and filed a motion for temporary guardianship. We were supposed to have a court date, but our motion was denied. We were told to file for full guardianship, which we did. Our court hearing was originally scheduled for April 2012.

In the meantime, Vegas kept my mother isolated, making it very difficult for Harold and me to see her. Even worse, she took advantage of my mother's dementia by spoon-feeding her lies about us and convincing her to believe them.

Then, the day before our scheduled court date, my attorney called to tell me that Vegas' attorney had filed a motion for a jury hearing (up to that point, our case was scheduled to be heard before a judge only). That changed everything. We had to get another court date. The earliest opening on the court's calendar was in September.

It was nothing more than a stall tactic, and

Harold and I knew it.

My attorney suggested that the best thing to do was to have a meeting with all of us: Vegas, her attorney, my mother, my mother's attorney (who had been assigned to her by the court), my attorney, and me. We all agreed to convene at my mother's apartment.

I did not have a good feeling about this, however. My suspicions were confirmed when, as soon as I arrived and tried to say hello to my mother, Vegas rushed to her side and said to her, "You don't have to talk to them. You don't have to listen to them. You don't have to do anything. Everything will be fine."

That set the tone for the rest of the meeting.

At one point, Vegas' attorney said that he had interviewed my mother for four hours and found that she "was extremely competent about everything."

"How would you know that?" I asked. "You don't even know her. You don't know her or her personality or anything about her."

"Well, she was very coherent," he insisted.

"You can be coherent and still not be competent," I said.

My attorney did everything he could to keep me calm. But things were not going well.

Then Vegas said, "You know why I did this? I did this because you were going to throw me out."

Ah, now it was clear to everyone in the room: This had nothing to do with the best interests of my mother. It was all about the money and Vegas looking out for herself.

She even brought up the time, a few months earlier, when Harold and I came by to take my mother to the doctor. (That was also the day, as you'll recall, when my mother was diagnosed with dementia.)

"You came here and you took her and you threw her in the wheelchair," said Vegas.

"Excuse me," I said. "I didn't put her in the wheelchair—you did."

"Oh," she said. "That's right. I put her in the wheelchair."

Everyone in the room could clearly see that this person was not in control—she was not rational, not competent, not anything.

In a situation like this, where you have attorneys who don't even know the people involved, you would think they would do their homework. You would think they would talk to family members—people that knew my mother and knew Vegas, including me—and not just take the word of whoever is sitting there. But Vegas' attorney did not do that.

Meanwhile, as we inched closer to our court hearing in September, my mother continued to go downhill. Vegas kept her in a sedentary state: No visitors, no getting dressed, no letting her out of the house. It was pointless to try and move her, so I left it in God's hands.

Still, I could not help but notice that my mother, a woman who had spent her entire life manipulating people, had herself been manipulated by two of her own daughters—first Jersey, then Vegas. It was the definition of irony, and yet it was also sad.

* * *

One Sunday morning, a nurse with hospice called

to say that my mother had taken a turn for the worse. Harold and I went over there immediately. Vegas called her boyfriend to come over, apparently because we were there.

I sat with my mother for a couple hours. She was awake and very alert. We reminisced about the old days, talked about Hawaii, talked about everything. Finally, she began getting tired. So I told her, "When you see Dad"—meaning, of course, my father, who had passed when I was very young—"go with him."

She said, "OK."

Then I said goodbye, not knowing whether I would ever see her again. I added, "I'll see you in my dreams." She laughed. We left.

When we got home, I called my brother, Dallas. At this point, I hadn't spoken to him in a while because he had joined forces with the other manipulators in my family. (All my siblings sought my mother's approval and love. It was their Achilles heel.) I told him that if he wanted to see her, he'd better do it soon because things were not looking good. I gave him that courtesy.

That was Sunday. He went to visit her on Monday or Tuesday. Wednesday morning, around seven o'clock, he called me and said, "She's gone."

He told me that he was with her when she passed. (Apparently it had never occurred to him to call me, so I might be there, too.) He said that she spent most of her final hours with her eyes closed, fighting and yelling in agony.

Given how she had lived most of her life, I was not surprised to hear that.

* * *

When we opened my mother's accounts at the bank when she first moved to Texas, we put her money in a CD. Initially, it had been in a stock investment, but as this was 2008 (around the time of the crash of Wall Street), investments weren't doing well.

The bank administrator asked my mother, "Do you want a POD on this?"

"What's that?" she said.

"Paid on death."

"Yes," she said. "I want to put my daughter's name on that." By "my daughter," she meant me.

"Mom, you don't need to do that," I remember saying at the time. "I already have power of attorney." Besides, I'd been handling all of her affairs for the past fifteen years.

"No, we'll just do that," she said. She knew that, in doing that, I would carry out her requests. I was her executor and would ultimately be carrying out her wishes as she had stated in her will.

At the time of her death that CD was worth about $120,000. Both Vegas and Jersey wanted that money. But because my mother signed it over to me, they could not touch it.

That was the only saving grace in all of this.

CHAPTER SEVENTEEN
The Funeral

That day, Wednesday, the funeral home came by to pick up my mother's remains. Harold, my daughter and I then went to pay our last respects. One week later, her body was prepared and sent to Hawaii.

Meanwhile, it was up to me to coordinate her burial. Because Hawaii is an island, however, that was not easy to do—meaning, you can't just pick any date for a funeral. You have to wait. My mother passed in September, but we were not able to schedule her burial until the first part of October.

My mother had specific requests about her burial. I knew that, because I was with her when she made them. She wanted a pink casket—in fact, when she was alive, she often said, "At my funeral, I can see me looking down at my family and I'll be in my pink casket." She wanted to wear a particular pink dress that I had in my house for years. (It was the same dress she had worn at my daughter's wedding.) She wanted the funeral to be at Diamond Head, where the rest of our family is buried.

I managed to get the priest from St. Patrick's Church, where my parents were married (and where I was baptized), to perform the Mass. The service took place in the chapel at the cemetery. It was open air on the side.

Prior to the start of the service, my cousin's son, Keone, said that he and his little combo band wanted to perform Hawaiian music before the start of the Mass. He asked me if there were any favorite songs of my mother that I wanted him to play. One song that she and my father always sang when I was a child was "Goodnight Irene." (Irene was my mother's first name.) But, since that song was from the 1940s, Keone didn't know it. I had to sing it for him so that he could get the melody. Then, at the end of the Mass, he asked me to come up and sing the first few bars again so that he could carry the tune. So I did.

Playing "Goodnight Irene" at a funeral may not make any sense, but, in my mother's case, it bore great significance. One of the lyrics is "I'll see you in my dreams."

Ironically, that's what I said to my mother the last time I saw her.

Near the end of the service, just before the casket was closed for the final time, there was one moment that was both strange and yet very spiritual for all of us. The priest invited all of the family members to come up to the casket and say the Lord's Prayer. As he did that, a bird flew in from the front door of the chapel and zoomed like a jet over the entire length of the walkway leading up to the altar. When it finally reached the casket, the bird made a complete circle above the casket before flying right back out the front door. At which point, the priest looked up and said, "There she goes."

It was as if my mother had been watching the entire proceedings and finally made her exit.

* * *

The next day, after my mother was cremated, we buried her urn in the ground with her father (my maternal grandfather). Harold and I stayed in Hawaii to handle a few final details, including the headstone. The cemetery had to make a new one with the names and dates for both my grandfather and my mother.

I understand and feel sad about the unfortunate circumstances that continue to shadow each of my four siblings. Unfortunately, I have had no contact whatsoever with any of them since my mother's funeral.

Because I was older than the rest of my siblings, my mother always put me in the position of taking care of them. I suppose that made me "different" in the eyes of my siblings—as if I was ultimately not one of them. That may have something to do with why we've remained estranged.

The irony, of course, is that I went through the same experience they did.

If there is any difference between my siblings and me, it's this: The abuse they suffered at the hand of my stepfather, and my mother's neglect to stop him, both caused significant psychological damage to each of them throughout their lives. I was fortunate to escape that kind of damage because I had help from a "higher source" that none of my siblings had.

Unlike the rest of my siblings, I remember having a loving relationship with my birth father prior to the abuse I endured under my stepfather. (I didn't have many years with my father, but I cherish the few memories I do have.) As a result of that experience, I also had a loving relationship with God. That relationship, from the time I was young, is what got me through.

I'll say it again. What about the abused children? Who cares about what has or will happen to them? They are the future of our world.

CONCLUSION

I have often wondered what my role in life is. I believe we all have a purpose. Was my abuse the basis of mine?

Children who have been abused have difficulty separating their emotions from their intellect—i.e., they do not know what is really right. This is why you have children who still love their parents, even though their parents abused them. The child's mindset is initially based on fear of their abuser and the threat the abuser poses. They believe what their abuser tells them to believe. Before long they realize how alone they really are. They witness the power and control that the abuser has over the people around him. That makes it terribly difficult for abused children to come forward as they get older.

Then there's the fear of what will happen to the abused child if he or she comes forward: *Where will I go? What will happen to my family?* For many children, that fear of the unknown is even more terrifying than the abuse itself.

People tend to see and perceive what they want to see and perceive. Some pundits claim that an abused child "could have done something," as if they had options. Having lived with sexual abuse in my younger years, I can tell you unequivocally that people who actually believe that victims "have options" haven't a clue.

Speaking on behalf of abused children, the abuse they experience does not end even if they try to come forward. Instead, it only just begins.

Abuse is one thing. Having to endure how our society perceives abuse is another.

Until I wrote this book, I've pretty much kept my life private. A life like mine is not something I'd want to share with everyone. Sexual abuse is as prevalent today as it was when I was young. So why does our society allow it?

There is no one "demographic" for sexual abuse of children. It happens in homes across the board. Children are warned about talking to strangers—but, more often than not, their abusers are family members, friends, and others whom they were supposed to trust. This is a sensitive subject that needs to be addressed.

For most sexually abused children, the fear that gripped them in childhood also never leaves them, even as they get older. Ashamed about what happened to them, they will never reveal it to anyone, for fear of how others will react.

Most people meet and judge others viscerally. If someone has never revealed anything so traumatic before, once they do start to unload they often become a jumble of emotions. Sometimes, in opening up about what happened to them, they can seem irrational, rambling and jumping from one point to another. That can make the person listening to them become very uneasy, even if they want to help them. For the victim, it's easier to say nothing than to be left so vulnerable.

Victims have to believe that God is always available to help them, even though they can't see Him. This is the mystery of life and God. Spirituality is essential.

Still, sometimes I wonder how God views sexual child abuse—or any kind of child abuse, for that matter.

I particularly wonder how God handles the abuse of children that took place at the hands of priests in the Catholic Church. Though many people knew what was going on, it remained covered up for a very long time. Were it not for the persistent efforts of a group of reporters who dared to expose the church, this story may never have come to light. Only then was credibility established for victims and they began to come out.

What is it about our society that does not recognize the long-term effects of abusing children? Children are extremely vulnerable at a young age and can be molded as a result of their circumstances.

Taking advantage of the defenseless and vulnerable is an atrocity in the eyes of God. Yet man continues to do it.

* * *

As I look back at the long-term effects of my life, I know how fortunate I am to have fared better than my siblings. I was born, encountered three and a half years of a normal life, was thrown into thirteen years of turmoil, endured nine years of tribulation, then another nine years of growth and learning until I married my current husband. We have been married nearly thirty-eight years as I write these pages and he continues to be the best part of my life.

I am now dealing with the physical effects as a result of all I endured in the early part of my life, but at least I know why my nervous system has been compromised. I have had years of medical issues, including digestive issues of one sort or another. Only in recent years did I realize that this was related to my past.

I did not let my mother's failure or my stepfather's abuse define me. For those who have been abused, I encourage you, "DO NOT LET YOUR ABUSE DEFINE YOU!"

As for my siblings, each of them has experienced a lot of turmoil in their lives over the years and they never had a chance to live the lives they may have wanted. The psychological damage of experiencing abuse from childhood into adulthood had its imprint.

There are many things I did not put in this book out of respect for my siblings. Everything that transpired for them in life was a result of their abuse.

* * *

While watching *Entertainment Tonight* one night, I heard Nancy Grace say, "I've never had a sex molester case where the mother sided with the child." That statement not only resonated with me, but made me think of my mother.

I'm curious how many victims are out there. My mind tells me maybe it's not as bad as I think, but my heart tells me the sheer number is probably unimaginable.

With all the advancements we've made as a society, why has sexual abuse of children remained so prevalent in so many families today? I hope that, by sharing my story, I can somehow make a difference.

A SPIRITUAL REFLECTION

I have always been a spiritual person. But, at this point in my life, I don't understand what God asks of me. He says honor thy father and mother and not to judge others. Given the history of my life, those are all difficult requests. But it also speaks to one of the reasons that brought me to write this book.

How is that, out of five children, only one manages to succeed in living life, while the others only exist in it? What factor led that one child beyond the other four?

Life is a perplexing journey. Are there spiritual influences that enable us to endure such a life?

I was born into the world of a dysfunctional family. We five children were subjected to a devastating childhood of abuse by a mother and stepfather (or, in the case of my two half-sisters, father). Our mother, out of insecurity or ignorance, made no apparent effort to protect us from our abuser.

When it comes to your mother, you will always

feel a bond, even if you cannot relate to who she is. She will always be a part of you, even if she was not a good mother. So when God says honor your mother and father, I don't believe He is saying that we have to accept our parents regardless of what they do. Rather, it's up to us to do for them what we can, despite themselves.

That is what I did with my mother. The end of her life did not go well, but looking back I don't think it was meant to.

My faith and trust in God have saved me from the unhappiness that has burdened my four siblings. No doubt about it. From infancy to adulthood, God had a hand in my life. I decided early on that my mother and stepfather would not destroy me and I would succeed in spite of them. I lifted myself from that life—and though I stumbled many times in my years as a young adult, somehow my faith in God always lifted me. It's been an undeniable journey with even more unbelievable results.

We try to follow what we think is the right road in life. Even so, sometimes when we find the right path, the outcome may be quite different than what we had expected.

God is essential in my life. This is not a cliché, but a fact. I could not have lived my life without His guidance. Many angels guided me in one form or another, and I am always aware of their guidance.

The mystery of life and what lies beyond fascinates me. I've always had a desire to read and study that subject. Oddly enough, those closest to me in and out of my family share that same desire. Is that a coincidence? I don't think so.

People are put in our lives for a reason. No one

knows that better than me. The relationships I have with these individuals were instantaneous at the time we met. Some people come into our lives right when we need them, but then we move on and they move on. Other friends come into our lives and remain connected with us until the end of the earth—and I believe they stay with us even beyond this world.

I am beyond grateful for what God has provided in my life, both good and bad. My connection to him can never be broken or altered. Through everything that's happened in my life I never blamed God, but I did blame man. Though God's plan is always there, man's free will often alters that plan. All any of us can do is have faith and trust that God is helping. That is what I've always done.

I never doubted God. I doubted myself at times (and consequently made the wrong decision during those times), but He always guided me back to His plan.

God put people in my life to help me and also for me to help:

My oldest friend, Myra, was my refuge as a child.

My loyal friend Joycelene was always there for me. We shared so much laughter together along with her brother, Emil. We've discussed, rehashed and solved the world's problems.

My spiritual friend, Mary Jo, were each other's psychologist and counselors.

My cousin Laverne and I share an unshakable faith in God. We bonded as children, were separated by man, and reconnected as adults. We've helped each other understand this journey that we're on in God's eyes. *Now faith is being sure of what we hope for and certain of what do not see.* Hebrews 11:1

Last of all is my husband Harold. In spite of workplace demands, problems with kids, etc. we have hung in there and have a very happy and loving life. He has supported me and encouraged me in writing this book.

I have many more supportive and wonderful friends in my life that have touched me in many different ways. I am forever grateful and blessed by their support and friendship.

Given what has transpired, I believe God is weaning me from toxic relationships. Some things in this life simply cannot be fixed. I have reached that serene place in life and I'm moving on.

In writing this story, I truly hope to help someone else know that, no matter what has happened to them, they will be okay and life can be good.

God put this Bible verse in my path at a very appointed time, August 1, 2015:

Can a mother forget the baby at her breast
And have no compassion on the child she has borne?
Though she may forget, I will not forget you!
See I have engraved you on the palm of my hands;
Your walls are ever before me.

Isaiah 49:15, 16

A PSYCHOLOGICAL PERSPECTIVE
by
Barbara Chase-Hopkins, LCSW
Licensed Clinical Social Worker

Child sexual abuse is very hard for most of us to understand, more so because it is often perpetrated by someone known to the victim of a member of their own family. When it is a member of their own family, that disturbs the very foundations of trust in relationships. A child develops their first sense of trust by having parents who treat them with respect, love, and consistency. According to Erik Erikson's Stages of Development, the stages of childhood in normal child development are as follows:

Birth to age 1	Trust vs. Mistrust
Age 2 to 3	Autonomy vs. Shame and Doubt
Age 4 to 6	Initiative vs. Guilt
Age 7 to 12	Industry vs. Inferiority
Age 13 to 19	Identity vs. Role Confusion

When a child is abused by a family member, the ensuing disturbance in trust will have repercussions in all future relationships for the rest of the child's life. When the abuse is sexual in nature, both the foundations of intimacy and trust are disturbed and the child grows up to be an adult who is unable to trust and have healthy intimate relationships. Many times, this results in the adult victim marrying an abuser and the dysfunction perpetuates itself from generation to generation.

The seriousness of child sexual abuse and its effect on the victim through adulthood cannot be overstated. Let's say that a child is sexually abused at the age of five. If the abuser is a parent, and the child's development was fairly normal up to that point, the child is traumatized and their sense of Trust vs. Mistrust is challenged. The child regresses back to the Trust vs. Mistrust stage of development to attempt to repair the damage done so that healthy development can continue.

If the other parent believes the child and the family receives good counseling, the child can repair the damage, and with time, regain their sense of trust. At this point, the child can return to the developmental stage at which the interference occurred.

However, if the child is not believed—or represses the abuse and tells no one—unless the parent protects the child and gets help for the family, the chances of the child being able to repair the damage and return to normal development are greatly reduced. In fact, what often follows is that the child grows up to be an adult who is still attempting to repair the damage to the Trust vs. Mistrust issue. This is done, unconsciously, by becoming involved with a series of people who, though they may seem charming initially, cannot be trusted. Then they attempt to change that person into someone who can be trusted in the hopes of attaining reparation.

Victims of sexual abuse also tend to handle their trauma in one of two ways. They become promiscuous and have little, if any, filter on their sexual activity, or they become withdrawn and unable to tolerate sexual intimacy. While it is possible to get lucky in one's choice of partners, for the most part, this is a cycle that is doomed to failure. Sadly, unless there is some intervention or therapy that helps that person work through the abuse, he or she will remain stuck in the Trust vs. Mistrust stage for a lifetime. Relationships either do not last or are characterized by disappointment (which results in hurt, anger, and more abuse). Attempts to self-medicate with drugs and/or alcohol are also a common characteristic of teens and adults who are sexually abused as children. These unstable adults tend to have children who grow up to be unstable adults. The cycle of abuse continues from one generation to another.

What is little known outside of mental health circles is that the family is a system. Systems work to sustain themselves at all costs, much like a corporation, a church, the military, or any other institution. When the perpetrator is a member of the family, the family often colludes in the abusive situation. You may have siblings who agree to let the abuse continue unreported because it is not happening to them. Perhaps they have a false sense of safety and don't want to be responsible for sending their father or mother to jail. Or, as in the case in this book, you have multiple siblings being abused and the mother is colluding in the abuse so that she can maintain her marriage and financially support herself and her children.

It is very difficult to understand why a mother would look the other way or knowingly stay with a man who is hurting her children. This goes against the grain of everything we think and feel about a mother's role and attachment to her children. In most cases, the mother has come from a highly dysfunctional family herself and has been hurt, abandoned, or abused. Allowing her children to be abused is the price she has to pay for some false sense of security, both financially and emotionally.

In the author's case, the mother had just lost her husband and had three small children. She was seduced by a charming perpetrator, ten years her junior, who saw a chance to have two little girls to prey upon. Within a year she was married to the perpetrator. After the mother became involved with this man, she was not willing to risk the shame or a lack of financial security. She stayed in the marriage and colluded with her husband in the abuse of her children. When the author stood up to the stepfather and threw the pan at him (see Chapter 4), the mother made the author leave because the stepfather no longer wanted her there. The mother never gave any thought that the stepfather was at fault and that he should leave. The damage to the children in this situation constitutes a developmental interference that is almost impossible to repair. The children cannot count on either parent for a sense of safety, love, and protection. It is the saddest of abusing situations.

Let me state this again: The family is a system and system will do anything to sustain themselves. The author's stepfather was in the military—another institutional system. Much has been written lately about the higher than average incidences of abuse in military families. At the time this abuse took place, in the 1950s, if a child or wife wanted to report the sexual abuse of a child, there was very little, if any, support for the victims to get out of the situation or for treating the perpetrator. It was considered a private matter; the military or state police needed to stay out. Abuse was sanctioned in this setting.

However, there is no middle ground when children are hurt. It is the responsibility of every person on this planet to protect them. The military and many other institutions are trying to deal with their past failure to protect children. There are also policies and programs in place to help families as abusing situations occur.

A major problem in families where sexual abuse takes place is the enormous sense of shame felt by every member of the family. Shame is almost always destructive because it goes so deep and it causes people to not want others to see who they really are. So they pretend and keep secrets—two things that will impede any kind of real relationship with others. So, these children become adults and remain emotionally isolated, lonely, and feel misunderstood and unlovable. They find each other and try to have relationships. These unhealthy relationships are often disastrous for everyone involved.

I know the author of this book and she has made a good life for herself. Why is that? The answer is worth further study. The author had a relationship with her biological father. She has traces of memory of that relationship. Many of these memories were around attending Mass with him and served as the foundation of her belief in God. So, when her stepfather began abusing her, the author had a memory of a trusting relationship with a father and she had a significant relationship with a heavenly Father. She was aware that the abuse was wrong and told her mother on several occasions throughout the years. She knew that her stepfather's behavior was inappropriate, and she did not feel responsible for the abuse. That is a remarkable epiphany to have for one so young.

Small children are very egocentric and tend to think that everything happens because of them. Though I am sure the author felt shame, her anger toward her stepfather was stronger and this "sense of herself" caused her to rebel against his abuse. As a result, she was the target of her mother's insecurities for the remainder of her mother's life.

Until she was fourteen, the author assumed she was the only daughter being abused. Then she saw her stepfather talking with her sister and her sister's reaction of looking down. That was when the author knew that her sister was being abused, too. She assumed that her abuse and the abuse of her sister were because they were not her stepfather's biological children. The abuse was eventually reported and the daughters were removed from the home for one year and sent to live with the stepfather's mother in Texas. The reporting of the abuse and the removal of the girls was the first time that the author was aware that her stepfather was also abusing his biological daughters.

At the end of one year, the author was old enough to emancipate, and she did so. That saved her. Her sister and her half-sisters had to go to Japan with the mother and stepfather, where the abuse continued until each of these girls was old enough to emancipate. As a result, all of the author's siblings felt abandoned by the author because she got out of the abusing situation—and they felt she left them in it. The author was the eldest, and in their eyes, the protector of her sisters—a perception that her mother encouraged. Of course, she was only eighteen and was living in Texas, while they were in Japan. Still, this "abandonment" caused a disturbance in their relationships that continues to this day.

The lost child in all of this was the one boy child, who was the author's brother and a stepson to the stepfather. The stepfather was not interested in him for obvious reasons, while the mother does not appear to have been very interested, either. When the girls were removed from the home and sent to Texas, the boy ran away from home. The parents told the police and had him returned. However, he did not accompany the family to Japan and went on to make a life for himself at the age of sixteen in Texas. The entire family eventually lost touch with him. Approximately twenty years later, the author made an effort to find him and the family was reunited. He did not have an easy life, but he had managed the best he could. So, even though this child was not the victim of abuse, he was aware of what was going on and could not stop the abuse of his sisters. He had survivor guilt and his role in the family was so skewed that his Initiative vs. Guilt and Identity vs. Role Confusion stages were never completed.

All three of the girls married whoever was available to help them escape from the abuse. They have all continued to be stuck in the first three stages of child development, and have had unhappy lives filled with drama and pain. The author had a child, made some friends, and got on her feet. She left her first husband, whom she had married out of need. She worked her way through her Identity vs. Role Confusion stage and went on with her life.

It bears repeating that the author's ability to do this, after what she had been through, was pretty remarkable. Perhaps she was lucky in her choice of a spouse when she remarried and was able to face and put behind her the abuse through his trustworthiness and loving support. But there is something else.

Mental health professionals have long been puzzled by how children can go through horrible childhood abuse and neglect and some of them make it through with less damage than others when all other factors seem equal. I do not know the answer, but somehow I believe that this speaks to the strength of an innate human spirit in some people that gives them the "sense" of options and resilience to move forward no matter what.

When the family returned from Japan, and after all of the girls had left home, the stepfather became a merchant seaman and traveled to the Far East on a regular basis. He impregnated a younger teenage girl. He waited until the girl was of age in the Asian country, married her, and brought her and their young son to the United States. The author's mother learned about the young girl and her son, and she finally divorced the stepfather. He lives in another state with his wife, his son, and another son and daughter born here in the States. And the cycle continues.

After completing her undergraduate degree in psychology, Barbara Chase-Hopkins worked at Therapeutic Intervention Program for Children for six years. The program worked with children age three to eight who had difficulties with learning and behavior that prevented them from going to public schools. After graduate school and a fellowship at Baylor College of Medicine in Child Psychiatry, Ms. Chase-Hopkins went into private practice, specializing in work with children age three to twelve. After twenty years in private practice, she retired and went to work part-time in her neighborhood elementary school as the school social worker for eleven years. Today she is happily retired.

Addendum:
Erik Erikson's Stages of Development

Stage	Age	Crisis to Overcome	Virtue to Attain	Description	Freudian Equivalent
1	0-1	Trust vs. Mistrust	Hope	At this stage, babies learn to trust that their parents will meet their basic needs. If a child's basic needs are not met, he or she might grow up with a general mistrust of the world.	Oral
2	2-3	Autonomy vs. Shame and Doubt	Will	As toddlers, children begin to develop independence and start to learn that they can do some things on their own (such as going to the toilet). If a child is not encouraged properly at this age, he or she might develop guilt over their needs or desires.	Anal
3	4-6	Initiative vs. Guilt	Purpose	As preschoolers, children continue to develop self-confidence through learning new things. If a child is not able to take initiative and succeed at appropriate tasks, he or she might develop guilt over their needs and desires.	Phallic
4	7-12	Industry vs. Inferiority	Competence	Throughout their school years, children continue to develop self-confidence through learning new things. If they are not encouraged and praised properly at this age, they may develop an inferiority complex.	Latent

5	13-19	Identity vs. Role Confusion	Fidelity	When they reach the teenage years, children start to care about how they look to others. They start forming their own identity by experimenting with who they are. If a teenage is unable to properly develop an identify at this age, his or her role confusion will probably continue on into adulthood.	Genital
6	20-34	Intimacy vs. Isolation	Love	During early childhood most people fall in love, get married and start a family. If a person is unable to develop intimacy with others at this age (whether through marriage or close friendships), they will probably develop feelings of isolation.	Genital
7	35-64	Generativity vs. Stagnation	Care	This is the longest period of a human's life. It is the stage in which people are usually working and contributing to society in some way and perhaps raising their children. If a person does not find proper ways to be productive during this period, this will probably develop feelings of stagnation.	Genital
8	65+	Integrity vs. Despair	Wisdom	As senior citizens, people tend to look back on their lives and think about what they have or have not accomplished. If a person has led a productive life, they will develop a feeling of integrity. If not, they might fall into despair.	Genital

Descriptions courtesy UsefulCharts.com

A SPIRITUAL PERSPECTIVE
by
Father Ed

The author in this story held on to a faith in God beyond her understanding. Where did this faith come from? Could it be that God and the Holy Spirit resided within her? Or did her father become her Guardian Angel?

Because we are privy to only certain aspects of this life and what lies beyond, all we can do is speculate.

It was never in God's plan for children to be abused in any way. Man's free will, however, can alter that plan. God does not do bad things, but man does.

The author in this story saw God as her mentor and savior. From a very young age, she had a sense of trust in God and prayed for His help continually and believed He was always with her.

Again we can only wonder where she got that belief. All we know is that she trusted in God and never wavered in her faith that He would somehow help her.

One of the great mysteries of this life is that God does not always help us in the manner we think He should. Rather, He works in different ways and in a different time frame than we expect. And though the author faced moments of great difficulty along her journey, she never doubted or blamed God for her life such as it was.

Let's look at the condensed version of the life of the author:

1. A four-year-old child is confronted by her predator. She instinctively has feelings and thoughts of what she must do to endure. She is on constant alert in order to avoid confrontation with him.

2. As time goes on, and she gets older, she relies on her belief in God, trusting everything will be okay. She concentrates on school and church.

3. As an adult, with no help from her family and with no mentors of her own, she learned to overcome her circumstances with the faith and trust she had.

Essentially God provided her with three major things to help her: *intuition*, *strength*, and *perseverance*. And there lies the answer of where her faith and strength came from.

A PERSPECTIVE
ON THE PHYSICAL HEALTH OF
PEOPLE WHO HAVE BEEN ABUSED
by
Dr. Eric Lewis

As a naturopathic physician, my practice is shaped by six core principles that guide my recommendations to my patients:

1. First, do no harm
2. Identify and treat the root cause of disease
3. Treat the whole person
4. Prevention
5. Doctor as teacher
6. The healing power of nature

from The American Association of Naturopathic Physicians
http://www.naturopathic.org/content.asp?contentid=59

Regardless of what ailments a person has, or what diagnosis they have been given, the art of naturopathic medicine involves understanding how these guiding principles apply to the unique individual sitting in front of me. If a person has suffered abuse, whether in their past or in more recent times, several of these principles can directly illustrate how strongly abuse can shape health.

It should go without saying that any relationship should involve no harm. However, abuse is all too common and can take many forms: physical, mental, emotional, psychological, or sexual. We have an intake form for our patients to fill out when they begin working with our practice. One of the questions asks if they have ever been subjected to abuse. I am saddened to say that, all too often, the answer to this question is yes.

When you think holistically about health, and when you really want to get to the bottom of an issue, you must consider what the root cause of illness is for someone. We are all unique beings, shaped by our environments and our relationships. Your collective experience will shape and mold you, for better or worse, and make you who you are today. I do believe that people are innately strong and resilient and are capable of handling a great deal of stress. At the same time, I see abuse as a root cause of disease.

Abuse that occurs to a child, or a teen, can deeply impact a person's overall health. In particular, the nervous system will often show signs of imbalance. Hypersensitivity, irritability, anxiety, depression, insomnia, and headaches are a few of the many symptoms that I see in victims of abuse. It's like the nervous system has innately learned to respond to its environment quickly or defensively.

That makes sense, when you think about it. Nervous system patterns and connections can take shape due to abuse, yet they can carry on for years or decades after resolution. As a result, treating a person who has suffered abuse should involve the whole person.

Learning and understanding just how abuse can affect a person as a whole is an essential tool in starting the path to well-being. Healing is absolutely possible, especially once we identify and treat the root cause of disease.

Dr. Eric Lewis
Lewis Family Natural Health, Inc.
info@lewisnaturalhealth.com

A MOTHER'S DAY MESSAGE
FROM MY DAUGHTER

Throughout my life, I have always tried to provide for my daughter, Denise, what I did not have as a child: as normal a life as possible. On Mother's Day 2016, she wrote a poem for me that expressed her gratitude and appreciation. Because this message says it all, I thought I'd share it with you.

> It's always been so clear to see
> That you were meant the MOM for ME
>
> When I was young we had just us
> At many times it seemed so tough
> Without your family to help us out
> You proved to me without a doubt
> That with your prayers and faith in God
> We'd both be strong and beat the odds
> Your friends were here for love and support
> But most of all for laughs of sort

COMPROMISED

We felt well balanced the two of us
A Mother, a Daughter, a bond with trust
Then one day you met a Man
Who'd ask you for your hand in hand
He changed our lives as we would see
Your love, your friend, and Father to me
You knew your prayers were answered then
But still continued to follow God's plan
I've watched you grow my independent Mom
And cherish your teachings that make me strong.

You share and care and give it your all
Bigger than life for being so small
You've taught me what a Mother stands for
And paved the way for me to soar
I too became a Mother-to-be
With a beautiful Daughter, like you and me
With all the love I hold in my heart
You provide me well from the very start

That's why it's been so clear to see
That you were meant the MOM for ME
I love you very much, Denise

A LETTER TO MY MOTHER
November 17, 1917
September 12, 2012

The life you led has had many repercussions that affected each of your children. I have to believe you did the best you could. I can't say the same for your children. I am sorry that I was not able to protect you from the difficult end of life you encountered, but negative forces prevailed and prevented me from doing what was in your best interest. God knows what was in my heart and what I wanted for you and now I hope you know as well. I will carry out your final wishes and I will honor you in a way that will hopefully be pleasing to both God and you.

I pray for you and may you finally be at peace.

A LETTER TO A CHILD MOLESTER
RYB

I often thought of what I should say if given the opportunity to face you again. I'm sure you never imagined it would be in this manner.

A man you are not, not even remotely close. You destroyed the growth and development of so many young girls. I know first-hand of three, my siblings, two of which are your own daughters. I, on the other hand, was given a strength and knowledge beyond my comprehension to deal with you, where my mother failed.

I know you have three other children, two boys and one girl. I pray those boys are nothing like you and I can only imagine the life your other daughter had to endure. No telling how many children you violated over the years. A legacy I'm sure you are proud of. Having the relationship I have with God, I sleep easy, knowing your day is coming.

The book is an attempt to help those who have been violated by child predators like yourself. The pen can be mightier than the sword, which is why I felt you needed a copy of this book so you can read about your successes. Read it and weep, for you have created a terrible injustice.

STATISTICS ON SEX OFFENDERS
Source: StatisticBrain.com

According to the website StatisticBrain.com, there are approximately 747,408 registered sex offenders in the United States as of this writing.

The states with the highest rates of sex offenders are Delaware (517 registrants per 100,000 people), Oregon (473 registrants per 100,000 people), Vermont (468 per 100,000), Michigan (403 per 100,000), Arkansas (396 per 100,000), Wisconsin (391 per 100,000), Minnesota (316 per 100,000), and Florida (311 per 100,000). The states with the lowest rates are Pennsylvania (ninety-four registrants per 100,000 people), Maryland (136 per 100,000), New Mexico (140 per 100,000), Rhode Island (146 per 100,000), North Carolina (149 per 100,000), Connecticut (152 per 100,000), Washington, D.C. (160 per 100,000), and New Jersey (164 per 100,000). (A breakdown of registrants per state appears on pages 160-161.)

Of the 747,408 total registered sex offenders in the U.S., approximately 265,000 registrants, or roughly 35 percent, are under the supervision of a corrections agency. By extension, that means that nearly two out of every three registered sex offenders roam their communities without supervision.

The average number of years that a convicted sex offender serves of an eight-year sentence is just 3.5 years. Seven out of every ten convicted offenders will commit another crime upon their release from jail—though that crime will not necessarily be sexual in nature. Only 2.7 percent of sex offenders will commit another sexual crime after their incarceration. Sixty percent of those second offenses, however, occur while living in a supervised community.

Also according to StatisticBrain.com, in eight out of every ten sexual molestation cases where the victim was a girl, the perpetrator was someone that the girl knew. The corresponding figure in cases where the victim was a boy is 93 percent.

Number of Registrants
Reported by State/Territory

Source: ParentsforMegansLaw.org
https://www.parentsformeganslaw.org/public/meganReportCard.html

Below are the sex offender registry counts for each state including the years 2005 through March 31, 2016. Sex offender counts are as reported by state agencies.

One asterisk (*) indicates the sex offender count as reported on state Internet Registry

Two asterisks (**) indicate statistics from the National Center for Missing & Exploited Children

"NR" indicates No Report Received

"RP" indicates that the sex offender count is pending

According to ParentsforMegansLaw.org, certain states may have a decrease in numbers due to the reviewing of all offender records, while some active registrants have been moved to inactive status. ("Inactive" status may include sex offenders that are no longer required to register due to court order or expired status, as well as offenders that are incarcerated, deceased, or who have moved out of state.)

STATE	2005	2006	2007	2008	2009	2010	2011	2012	2013	2014	2015	2016
Alabama	5,616	5,193	8,943	9,745	10,675	13,329	13,293	12,000	12,912	13,371	14,098	14,209
Alaska	2,873	4,219	3,032	5,300	1,885	1,842	2,779	2,000	2,140	*3,212	2,246	2,246
Arizona	9,221	11,305	14,260	14,500	14,380	14,519	14,533	14,533	*14,500	15,018	15,438	15,438
Arkansas	5,864	6,426	7,612	8,099	9,219	10,151	8,996	11,474	12,919	*10,051	15,133	11,809
California	102,616	86,846	87,706	66,041	63,500	86,912	123,821	123,821	80,848	82,646	82,646	84,315
Colorado	8,381	9,125	11,369	9,961	6,950	10,980	14,666	15,240	16,098	16,919	17,717	17,915
Connecticut	3,785	4,106	4,725	4,769	4,950	5,078	5,341	5,427	**5,281	5,329	5,799	*5,795
District of Columbia	624	641	3,307	746	812	880	*926	*926	**995	980	*991	*1,004
Delaware	2,961	2,984	696	3,461	3,775	3,998	4,040	4,631	4,871	4,720	4,736	4,579
Florida	33,990	33,910	43,590	47,455	51,847	53,202	47,524	58,780	61,303	64,431	67,143	68,845
Georgia	8,958	11,744	14,257	15,293	16,391	18,811	20,371	21,559	23,147	25,693	27,500	27,912
Hawaii	1,957	2,170	2,382	2,500	2,843	2,934	3,404	3,342	**2,940	2,974	* 3,035	*3,027
Idaho	2,606	2,801	2,866	3,072	3,200	3,451	3,655	3,654	3,872	4,093	4,305	4,347
Illinois	17,100	17,890	23,749	19,695	23,604	21,007	21,317	28,206	22,406	23,240	23,651	23,755
Indiana	7,300	8,500	8,652	9,486	11,951	10,515	9,053	10,030	**14,585	11,194	*11,494	*11,378
Iowa	6,104	6,058	6,249	5,499	4,912	7,032	5,283	5,381	*5,797	5,860	5,289	5,324
Kansas	3,563	3,981	4,791	5,911	11,617	9,677	6,047	6,275	7,409	8,593	9,547	9,658
Kentucky	4,898	5,351	6,466	6,914	7,532	8,127	8,718	9,070	9,545	10,143	10,584	10,742
Louisiana	6,591	6,921	7,502	7,937	9,592	7,823	8,346	10,614	8,271	9,038	9,200	9,320
Maine	1,553	1,670	2,825	3,069	3,325	3,300	2,930	2,927	3,079	3,186	2,734	2,716
Maryland	4,253	4,340	4,668	5,810	6,112	6,545	7,177	7,807	*8,495	**8,734	7,063	7,063
Massachusetts	18,000	8,104	11,768	14,896	13,125	15,341	11,182	11,182	**11,307	11,449	11,502	11,448
Michigan	36,233	38,032	41,145	48,000	43,613	45,717	46,122	39,795	40,692	*37,887	42,071	38,753
Minnesota	15,819	13,885	14,097	20,336	14,714	15,875	16,207	16,948	17,541	17,376	17,777	17,845
Mississippi	3,300	3,689	4,562	4,888	5,440	6,088	6,777	7,027	**7,696	8,285	9,120	9,281
Missouri	10,719	11,031	7,324	6,996	7,284	11,226	12,194	12,707	13,442	14,424	15,256	15,322
Montana	3,370	1,495	1,697	1,746	1,798	1,971	2,111	2,131	2,296	2,374	*2,375	2,492
Nebraska	2,041	2,189	2,605	2,748	2,966	3,188	3,680	3,861	4,268	4,724	5,058	5,104
Nevada	4,734	5,573	6,082	6,386	6,479	6,553	6,832	6,671	7,188	6,361	6,628	6,629
New Hampshire	3,100	3,250	11,566	2,200	4,128	2,336	2,420	2,420	2,532	2,337	2,762	2,744
New Jersey	10,464	11,003	3,706	12,000	12,551	13,179	14,224	14,224	15,131	17,614	18,189	15,645
New Mexico	1,864	1,915	2,286	2,133	2,497	2,631	*2,808	2,950	3,505	3,966	3,551	3,570
New York	20,969	22,209	25,536	26,688	28,843	29,423	*30,284	33,716	35,810	37,816	*31,359	*30,968
North Carolina	10,244	9,228	12,140	12,167	14,342	12,831	13,554	14,321	14,828	19,984	*16,695	*16,870
North Dakota	801	946	1,037	1,277	2,980	2,616	*1,529	1,743	2,144	1,808	*1,763	*1,728
Ohio	13,485	13,750	17,669	16,902	19,394	18,616	29,546	19,141	18,022	18,870	*17,709	17,683
Oklahoma	5,507	5,118	9,633	3,664	6,790	6,563	6,907	7,170	7,701	5,994	6,200	6,266
Oregon	15,259	17,160	18,873	14,487	16,295	21,562	17,650	24,660	**18,930	27,546	28,530	28,736
Pennsylvania	7,199	7,736	9,362	9,730	10,194	10,021	11,236	11,846	**13,862	17,197	18,828	19,257
Rhode Island	1,640	1,352	1,753	1,659	365	1,645	1,499	1,528	1,579	1,613	1,674	1,680
South Carolina	8,049	8,556	10,095	10,621	11,470	12,295	*13,037	13,308	8,934	14,373	16,079	*15,138

South Dakota	1,707	1,993	2,398	2,467	2,788	2,688	2,861	2,976	3,132	3,323	3,436	3,475
Tennessee	7,873	8,561	10,500	11,513	13,122	11,796	15,210	18,537	19,562	20,861	21,680	21,907
Texas	46,484	44,336	50,559	52,574	57,105	59,105	67,707	71,124	77,693	82,224	86,217	87,149
Utah	8,000	6,904	7,181	6,900	7,350	7,997	*6,916	6,983	7,037	7,147	7,354	7,436
Vermont	2,226	2,340	2,443	2,447	459	2,461	*1,129	*1,129	1,441	1,863	1,341	1,349
Virginia	13,211	12,152	15,000	4,618	17,110	16,891	18,728	19,137	20,081	27,953	22,143	22,299
Washington	18,557	18,790	19,798	20,016	19,112	20,403	20,183	21,008	18,270	18,913	18,780	18,556
West Virginia	2,220	2,500	2,800	2,800	3,086	3,326	3,619	3,638	*3,534	3,798	4,591	4,618
Wisconsin	17,169	17,887	19,629	20,199	20,611	21,324	22,106	22,381	22,803	23,480	23,990	24,123
Wyoming	929	981	1,115	1,355	1,389	1,412	1,496	1,526	3,641	1,815	1,655	2,182
Puerto Rico	NR	NR	NR	NR	NR	2,155	*2,720	NR	3,246	2,886	*2,881	*2,836
American Samoa	NR	NR	NR	NR	NR	48	NR	NR	**149	NR	NR	**164
Guam	286	396	418	481	523	570	544	717	771	724	925	940
US Virgin Islands	NR	NR	NR	NR	NR	155	80	109	95	108	*119	114
Northern Mariana Islands	NR	NR	NR	NR	NR	NR	*49	NR	**55	80	89	*77

Total Registrants 551,987 541,242 614,424 602,157 636,940 690,073 745,367 772,785 722,358 796,598 808,676 805,781

ABOUT THE AUTHOR

A survivor of child sexual abuse, Barbara Jean August has, upon writing this book, dedicated the remainder of her life to advocating for the rights of abused children. She is retired and lives with her husband in the state of Texas.

Most of the proceeds from the sale of this book will support various child sexual abuse organizations in the United States.

Contact information:

Barbara Jean August
P.O. Box 9
Conroe, Texas 77305

b72jeanaugust@gmail.com
www.CompromisedtheBook.com